FAIR PLAY

Louise Hegarty

FAIR PLAY

PICADOR

First published 2025 by Picador
an imprint of Pan Macmillan
The Smithson, 6 Briset Street, London EC1M 5NR
EU representative: Macmillan Publishers Ireland Ltd, 1st Floor,
The Liffey Trust Centre, 117–126 Sheriff Street Upper,
Dublin 1, D01 YC43
Associated companies throughout the world
www.panmacmillan.com

ISBN 978-1-0350-3613-4 HB
ISBN 978-1-0350-3614-1 TPB

1 3 5 7 9 8 6 4 2

A CIP catalogue record for this book is available from the British Library.

Map artwork by
Typeset by Palimpsest Book Production Ltd, Falkirk, Stirlingshire
Printed and bound by CPI Group (UK) Ltd, Croydon, CR0 4YY

Visit **www.picador.com** to read more about all our books
and to buy them. You will also find features, author interviews and
news of any author events, and you can sign up for e-newsletters
so that you're always first to hear about our new releases.

For Mom, Dad and Martha

PART ONE

IT'S THAT TIME OF THE YEAR AGAIN
WHERE WE CELEBRATE
BENJAMIN'S BIRTHDAY, RING IN
THE NEW YEAR,
AND SOLVE A MURDER!

YOU ARE CORDIALLY INVITED TO A
MURDER MYSTERY NIGHT THIS NEW YEAR'S EVE
TO CELEBRATE BENJAMIN'S BIRTHDAY.

PLEASE ARRIVE AT 2 P.M.

DRESS IS JAZZ AGE DETECTIVE.

LOCATION: YEW TREE HOUSE.
DIRECTIONS ATTACHED.

PLEASE RSVP TO ABIGAIL

*

Abigail wakes at seven, stretches, does ten minutes of tepid meditation, showers, dresses, does her skincare and make-up routine, dries her hair, makes scrambled eggs on half a bagel with some hot sauce, hauls the suitcase she had packed last night into the boot of her car and then gently places the champagne, wine and food into the back seat. She ticks items off her to-do list and checks her watch. She makes sure that she has the receipt for the cake in her bag and then double-checks the route to the bakery on her phone – it should take her twenty-eight minutes without traffic.

She arrives at the bakery a little before opening time and while she's waiting, she looks over the messages from the Airbnb hosts confirming the time of her arrival. She watches as the minute hand ticks slowly towards the hour. The moment the door is unlocked, she is out, receipt in hand. The cake is boxed and ready and she places it carefully on the floor of the car. She inputs the Eircode of the Airbnb into Google Maps, presses play on a podcast and thinks about everything she has to do before the others arrive later in the afternoon. Abigail is the organizer of the group: a role that she both enjoys and resents in equal measure.

The roads are quiet and as she goes through her mental checklist, the car moves swiftly from city street to dual carriageway and then finally onto a narrow rural road. She turns off the podcast so that she can concentrate fully on driving. Continue on for three kilometres. Turn right at the stop sign. In two kilometres bear left.

At a crossroads, she slows to a stop. On her right there is a row of houses, a small shop and a pub advertising rooms for rent. On her left is a petrol station. She makes her turn and proceeds to drive up a narrow curving road. A family out for a walk wave at her. An approaching car pulls into a layby to let her pass. And then eventually, the voice on her phone announces that she has arrived at her destination.

She drives through the large pillars, past the vacant gate lodge and up the tree-lined driveway. The house is up ahead – ivy-covered and facing southwards. She imagines that in spring or summer the grounds are verdant and fertile. The paved driveway turns to gravel under the wheels of her car, and she parks in front of the house next to an old Jeep. The house is situated on the brow of a hill, fields tumbling down in front and then rising again on the other side of the valley. Other houses are dotted here and there in the distance. As she gets out of her car, the front door opens, and a man and a woman appear. They are maybe in their mid-sixties. They both have glossy grey-speckled hair and are wearing padded gilets and jeans. 'You must be Abigail,' the woman says. 'I'm Dorothy and this is Brian.' On the front step, Dorothy hugs her warmly and asks her about her drive down. 'It was a breeze without the traffic,' she says. Brian extends his hand to shake hers.

Abigail follows them through the heavy front door into the

entrance hall. 'Welcome to Yew Tree House,' says Brian. 'It was built in the early 1790s in the Palladian style before being extended in 1867. It then fell into disrepair when the last of the original family died. My parents bought it in 1954 on some mad whim and they spent decades renovating it until we took it over.' Abigail gazes up at the high ceiling with its delicate cornices and chandelier. She feels suddenly very small. 'It must have been magical growing up here,' she says and then immediately regrets it as it becomes obvious from the look on Brian's face that she has interrupted his monologue. 'I don't know about magical,' he says. 'It didn't always look this good. Most of my childhood was spent dodging buckets of water until my parents got the money together to fix the roof.' 'Oh, but even then . . . I mean . . . as a child . . . so many great hiding places, all the games you could play . . . so much scope for the imagination,' says Abigail. 'I think Brian was born middle-aged,' his wife says, laughing. 'The idea of play-ing hide-and-go-seek probably never occurred to him.' She squeezes her husband's arm playfully and he smiles in return. *How quickly she can soothe him*, thinks Abigail, *and how nice it must feel to enjoy the gentleness of a long marriage.*

Brian continues with the tour. To Abigail's left is the formal living room ('or drawing room if you're being fancy') and then down the corridor is the sitting room with bookcases lining the walls. Across the corridor is the study ('where my father smoked cigars after dinner'). Back in the entrance hall, Abigail is led past a grandfather clock and through to the other wing of the house where the dining room and kitchen are. 'We did it up about eight years ago so it's all very modern,' says Dorothy. 'That's the pantry and we put in this breakfast bar because we know that not everyone enjoys the formality of the dining room all the time.' Brian brings her through to what used to be the servants' quarters. 'We use the space as a utility room now,' he says, 'and for storage. If you need more chairs or a vacuum cleaner, you'll find those things in here.' A sliding door leads to a small courtyard with some seating, a firepit and a shed filled with expertly stacked firewood.

'We've had a couple of New Year's Eve parties here over the years,' says Dorothy, 'though we're a little old for that now.' 'It's half a New Year's bash,' explains Abigail, 'and then half a birthday party for my brother – he'll be thirty-three tomorrow.' Dorothy and Brian both make a pitying face. 'Oh god, the poor thing,' Dorothy says. 'What a bore to be born on New Year's Day. No one ever wants to do anything.' Abigail shrugs. 'I don't think he minds,' she says. 'He's happy not to be the centre of attention.' They go back into the entrance hall and head upstairs ('Take notice of the stained-glass windows with the family crest'). Abigail's eyebrows raise slowly.

'So, most of the bedrooms are quite similar in size . . . this is the main bathroom of course and the laundry in case you need sheets or pillows. There are two en suites including the master bedroom which is here on the right . . . and then . . . I need to show you . . .' Brian brings her into a small room painted a light yellow. On one wall is a mural of the house and its grounds in a previous century. It is protected behind a sheet of Perspex. 'This bedroom is smaller than the others,' he says, 'but it's a real gem. Personally, I think it has the best views but more importantly it is the only room that retains a fully intact wall mural by Nathaniel Grogan. A really remarkable piece.'

Back downstairs, they hand over the keys and Abigail

waves them off as their Jeep disappears down the driveway. She checks her watch. She has just under two hours before everyone starts arriving. It will be just enough time. Abigail unpacks the car, storing the food in the cupboard, hiding the cake for later and putting the champagne into the fridge to chill. She goes upstairs and checks the bedrooms, assessing and then mentally assigning them to each of the guests. She unpacks her small suitcase, checks the settings on the oven and then starts preparing for that night's festivities. This is her favourite part: hiding all the clues and red herrings around the house.

The first year they had held a murder mystery party she had been a little hesitant about the whole thing and so had just printed off pictures of objects (a gun, a will, a broken watch) and hidden them around the rental property: a nondescript family home. But with each year she was growing bolder. She had learned that the more effort she put in, the more people enjoyed it. And because they hadn't been able to do this in the past two years, she had decided to go all out. The house was more expensive than what they would usually have opted for but she felt they had all earned it.

She really enjoyed creating all the clues: a crumpled-up love letter made to look old by dipping it in tea like she'd done as a child; an old-fashioned ticket stub for a theatre perform-ance; and a cheap handkerchief which she had sewn initials on. Then there is the murder weapon itself: a champagne bottle to which she had carefully applied a set of fingerprint stickers. She hopes everyone appreciates the work she has put in. She wants very much to impress them.

She wonders whether she should change into her outfit

now in order to greet everyone when they arrive but decides that this might be a bit too much, a little try-hard.

The others are due to arrive at two and even though she knew they would be late she is still disappointed when they fail to show at the appointed time. She lies down on the sofa in the living room and starts to scroll through her phone: ticking items off her to-do list, checking the news and WhatsApp. She selects Stephen's profile and scrolls through the last few messages between them – a photo taken after a parkrun, a link to an article that might interest him, an exchange of Happy Christmases. Time flashes by. Fifteen minutes disappear and then another ten minutes without her even knowing.

At about half past two the doorbell rings and Abigail races out to find Barbara standing on the porch. Barbara is Benjamin's work friend, and this is her first time being invited to one of these parties.

Barbara is the only person who will be late on purpose and is stunned to find that nobody else has arrived before her. She thought that being half an hour late would be enough but apparently not. She clasps her small overnight bag in front of her tightly. 'Oh, I'm sorry,' she says with a nervous laugh when she learns that she is the first arrival. 'Did I get the wrong time?' 'Oh no, we just have a lot of friends who struggle with punctuality,' replies Abigail. She invites Barbara in, taking her bag from her and forcing her to participate in some small talk ('how was the drive down? how was Christmas? the weather has been very mild hasn't it?'). She gives her a short tour ('the drawing room, the study') and gabs on about the house ('this wing was added in the 1860s') before bringing her upstairs to her bedroom ('I should leave you to unpack').

Abigail retreats downstairs and Barbara proceeds to waste as much time as she can without seeming impolite. She takes out all her clothes and hangs them up one by one in the dark mahogany wardrobe. She places her pyjamas on her pillow. She sets out her skincare and make-up and hair things on the dresser. She checks her appearance in the mirror and pulls her black hair up into a casual ponytail. She stores her small bag underneath the bed. She checks her phone for a signal. She looks out the window at the long driveway and far-away fields and wonders if she was right to accept this invitation. Normally she wouldn't have. Normally she would have made some excuse and stayed at home out of politeness. She would have turned down the invitation for their sake. Sometimes you have to do that. But for some reason she said yes this time. So unlike her.

Eventually and reluctantly, she comes downstairs. Barbara offers to help with any chores, but Abigail won't let her. 'Oh no, you're a guest,' says Abigail so Barbara sits awkwardly at the breakfast bar while Abigail flits about.

Thankfully, she soon hears another car arriving and then Abigail's voice greeting people in the hallway and the rush of new voices. Barbara feels odd staying in the kitchen by herself, so she slowly ventures out. Her stomach tightens when she realizes that she doesn't recognize anyone. Still no Benjamin. Abigail is hugging and kissing the new arrivals. She turns to introduce them to Barbara: 'This is Cormac and Olivia. And this is Stephen.'

The house suddenly feels full of life: full of people and luggage and friendly voices. 'I feel a little out of place here,' says Cormac. 'This is too fancy for the likes of me.' Abigail leads the newcomers upstairs. She points Cormac and Olivia towards the room with the double bed and en suite as they are the only couple. Olivia recognizes and appreciates this act of hospitality. She is relatively new to the group and is eager to find her place. She likes Abigail. She thinks they could be good friends. The pandemic had made it difficult for everyone to get together and she hasn't yet been able to brush off that feeling of being an outsider. She has talked to Cormac about it, but he always acts a little hurt and says, 'aren't my friends always welcoming to you?' And of course, they are. They are polite and friendly in the way you are with a stranger. But Olivia doesn't want to be a stranger anymore. She is a little glad to see that Barbara is here – the only person newer than her.

Stephen has started unpacking in the room next door. 'No, not in here,' Abigail says in an exaggerated whisper. 'I've got a better room for you.' When she was younger, she had had a crush on Stephen. It had seemed so important at the time. She tells herself that she has grown out of it, though she is still happy when he tells her his partner has gone back to Poland for Christmas. 'I thought you might like the view,' she says. 'And the mural. It's over two hundred years old.' She touches her hand to the Perspex as Stephen throws his bag down on the bed and then himself down after it. 'The house is amazing, Abigail. Such a great find. It looks even bigger than in the photos you sent,' he says, propping himself up on his elbows. 'I haven't seen you in so long,' she says tentatively. 'I know, I know,' he replies. 'I suppose it's just work and relationships and pandemic shit. We should set up a regular thing in the New Year. You know, just the two of us or with Benjamin or whatever.' Abigail tries not to look too happy. 'Oh, let me show you my get up,' says Stephen.

She sits down on the bed as he rifles through his bag before finally emerging with a small hat: a deerstalker. 'For my big role as the Great Detective later on.' 'It suits you,' says Abigail as Stephen preens in front of the mirror. Stephen really enjoys these parties. He loves socializing and he loves people and drinking and having fun. He often feels constrained by his corporate job and doesn't feel like the bare facts of his life reflect who he really is. 'You know Sherlock Holmes never actually wore a deerstalker in the books,' Abigail adds, fiddling with the bedspread. 'That was just in the films and television series. People just associate it with him now.' 'I have some other props as well,' Stephen says, 'but I'm going to keep them a secret for now. I don't want to spoil the surprise.'

Downstairs, Barbara is back sitting at the breakfast bar wondering how much longer they will be. She gets herself a glass of water. She goes to the sliding door thinking she might go outside and explore or at the very least give the impression that she is doing anything other than waiting. She is saved from further awkwardness by the sound of another car arriving. Finally, the last guests have arrived.

Abigail rushes downstairs to open the front door and Declan barrels in, chucking his bags on the ground and hugging and kissing everyone aggressively, even Barbara, whom he has never met before.

Declan has known Benjamin since they were five years old, but over the years they have been slowly drifting apart. Unfortunately, the only person who hasn't realized this is Declan himself. And though he continues to be invited to certain events during the year, it has been a long time since he made sense in this room with this group of people.

Benjamin and Margaret follow behind him. Benjamin pauses at the door to allow Margaret to go through first. He is carrying both of their bags. 'You've cut your hair,' Margaret remarks as she hugs Abigail hello. After greeting Cormac and Stephen, Benjamin spots Barbara and smiles. 'Oh good, you've arrived,' he says. Abigail starts to take his luggage upstairs to his room for him. 'You don't have to do that,' he says, but Abigail places a hand on his shoulder and reminds him that he is the birthday boy. 'I know how much you enjoy all the fuss,' she says.

She goes upstairs and Margaret follows her. 'You'll have to give me the full tour,' says Margaret. 'I'm liable to get lost in this mansion.' Abigail asks about their drive down and Margaret says, 'oh it was fine', but Abigail feels as though the other woman isn't quite meeting her eyes. Benjamin and Margaret had dated in college and while their relationship had ended years prior, they had remained good friends. Abigail is about to ask her another question when Declan barges in. 'You're next door,' she tells him. When he sees the bedroom, he puts up a mild fuss. Somehow, he thought he would be sharing with Benjamin. 'Benj would want that,' he says. 'Like old times.' 'We've got a bigger house this year, so we all have our own rooms. I picked that one specially for you,' Abigail says, as though she is speaking to a child. Declan irritates her in ways she can't describe but also, she worries for him. Benjamin told her recently that Declan had been rejected for a mortgage because his frequent use of gambling apps had been revealed in his bank statements. She distracts

Declan with talk of low champagne stock, and he tosses his bag into his room and hurries away. Margaret rolls her eyes and Abigail has forgotten to ask her question.

Back downstairs, everyone has gathered in the kitchen. Cormac and Olivia are sitting at the breakfast bar, Barbara and Benjamin are both leaning against the countertop and Declan is examining the contents of the fridge. Stephen is looking out the sliding door at the courtyard. 'Where's the girlfriend?' Declan asks Stephen. 'Has she dumped you already?' He laughs but nobody else does. 'She went back to Poland for Christmas,' Stephen explains patiently. 'Poland? Oh, I thought she was from Latvia or somewhere, eh, Lithuania,' says Declan. 'Nope. She's from Poland which is why I said she was in Poland. That was the clue,' says Stephen. 'You know what they say about Polish wo—' But Declan is interrupted by Cormac. 'Okay, okay,' he says, getting up from his stool. 'It's a little early for this.' Declan has an innocent look on his face, but he doesn't put up a fight. Cormac suggests going for a walk before the night's festivities. 'C'mon,' he says. 'Before it gets dark.'

Everyone puts on their coats and heads down the driveway and onto the small rural road. Cormac and Olivia are up front with Declan just behind them on his phone. Abigail is walking with Margaret and Stephen. She glances behind to see Benjamin speaking quietly and gently with Barbara. There are no cars about, so they walk in the middle of the road. 'Did you have a nice Christmas?' Margaret asks, linking arms with Abigail as though they are sisters. 'Oh, just the usual,' Abigail says. 'Quiet.' Stephen jokes that today is the first day since Christmas Eve he has put on shoes. 'I wasn't expecting to do any exercise,' he says with a laugh.

Abigail asks Margaret about her new job which sounds very much like her old job, but she is happy about it. Her office has views over the river and a very good coffee machine. Margaret keeps glancing behind them. 'Barbara seems nice,' she says. 'Had you met her before?' Abigail looks at her keenly. 'Once. Benjamin says that she had a bad break-up with her boyfriend recently. I hope she enjoys herself tonight.' Margaret glances back again.

They round a bend and suddenly they can see the whole valley in front of them. Down below is the road they had all travelled on earlier, gently meandering towards the cross-roads. There is a single car parked at the petrol station.

A couple with two dogs are walking towards them, both with smiley red faces. 'Heya,' says Benjamin, getting down on his haunches to greet the dogs. 'You're lovely.' 'They're mutts,' says the woman, 'but they're our mutts if you know what I mean.' Benjamin asks their names and rubs their heads.

'Could you do us a favour?' asks Stephen. 'Would you mind taking a photo of us?' He presents his phone to the woman. 'You better give it to my husband. I'm not good with technology.' She takes the other leash from her husband and Stephen hands the phone to him. The group gathers together, and the man takes a step back to try to get them all in frame. 'You need to squeeze in more,' he says, indicating with his hands. Abigail is squashed up against Stephen. He puts his arm around her, drawing her in closer to him. Her head rests a little on his shoulder. 'Smile for the camera,' the man calls out and he takes the photo. 'You must be up at Yew Tree House,' he says as he hands the phone back to Stephen. 'Brian told us they had a group coming.' 'Do you live nearby?'

'We're neighbours – about two fields over.' 'They've put a lot of work into that house,' the woman says. 'They've spent a lot of money too,' says the man. 'Always attending auctions and fairs looking for furniture. They've done a lovely job on it.' They exchange Happy New Years before parting ways.

As they move on, Abigail notices Stephen rubbing his lower back. He tells her it's an injury he picked up in a recent five-a-side game. 'Your brother has bailed the last few weeks – probably too miserable for him – so as the only other decent player, I have been pushed to my physical limits,' he says. Cormac joins the conversation to share his own complaint of an injury. He pulls up his trouser leg and starts palpating his ankle, which he claims is swollen. Olivia, standing behind him, throws her eyes to heaven. 'Maybe you just have fat calves,' says Stephen. Cormac whips around to Olivia, who is trying to suppress a smile. 'Did she tell you to say that?' Cormac asks Stephen. Olivia is laughing openly now. 'It is swollen,' Cormac insists. 'You can see the skin . . .' But now there is more laughing and so he hastily rolls his trouser leg down again. Olivia pulls him into her and kisses him.

The road becomes a little narrower and the ditch on either side makes way for a stout stone wall. Across a bare field, there are the remains of a church. The gate opens easily for them, and they walk through the canopy of skeleton trees until they have reached the ruined abbey. They split up then, everyone exploring the various chambers and burial ground by themselves. It is calm here. A place of retreat. Abigail moves through the body of the church, her hand glancing against its limestone walls. In the graveyard, she bends down to examine the broken headstones and trace her fingertips along the grooves to try and decipher the names and dates. The gloaming light makes the place seem unreal. When she stands up again, she spots Benjamin – perfectly framed in a doorway – his hands dug into his pockets, his eyes closed, and his face turned skyward.

Eventually, they come back onto the road and start their walk back to the house.

By the time they reach the gates, the sun has set and the birds in the hedgerow have begun their dusk chorus. The gravel crunches under their feet and the light Abigail left on in the entrance hall welcomes them home.

*

Stephen and Cormac go fetch the firewood and begin to clean and prepare the firepit. Benjamin comes into the kitchen to ask Abigail if she needs any help, but she insists that he should relax. 'You don't have to keep an eye on me,' she says, giving his elbow a reassuring squeeze. He asks after Barbara, but Abigail tells him instead to help Cormac and Stephen light the fire and he reluctantly heads outside.

Declan hovers around, telling the girls about some apparently hilarious scandal at his workplace that sounds to Abigail like a serious assault. He offers to help but he clearly doesn't mean it and eventually he retreats to the living room to scroll through his phone. Abigail sets out the cheese plate and prepares the charcuterie and crackers. Olivia, on Abigail's instruction, starts making little canapés with pâté and tapenade and goat's cheese and some very expensive smoked salmon. The rest is party food from M&S which Abigail knows everyone likes. Someone has put on music and Abigail can feel herself relax. Her whole body melts, though that might also be the result of the drink someone has pressed into her hand. She can hear sounds from outside, as Benjamin, Cormac and Stephen attempt to light a fire. She can't hear exactly what they are saying but she enjoys the rhythm of their voices. She hears their laughter, then their frustration, and finally the victorious whoops as the fire eventually takes hold. Margaret is standing at the open door watching them and having a smoke.

When Benjamin appears from outside followed by Stephen and Cormac, it is time to go upstairs and change for the evening. New Year's is always themed, though Abigail isn't too strict: it could be country-house chic or Prohibition-era New York. This year it is Jazz Age detective. Abigail gets changed in a hurry – quickly putting her hair up, fixing her make-up and then slipping on her sequinned flapper dress. As she is zipping herself up, her phone vibrates. Stephen has sent on the photograph of them all from the walk. There's Olivia and Cormac crouching down in front, Benjamin hiding a little behind Barbara on the right, Margaret standing stiffly next to Declan and in the middle Abigail and Stephen. She pinches the screen to get a good look. She sees her own face, all bright-eyed and grinning madly, and feels a little embarrassed.

She finishes zipping herself up, puts on her shoes and then goes and knocks on Benjamin's door. She lets herself in with-out waiting for a response. He is sitting on the edge of the bed tying his shoelaces and he looks up as she enters. 'Oh, you're wearing the earrings,' he says. He had bought them for her for Christmas. 'I want to check out your balcony,' says Abigail, and she unlocks the door and steps outside. The billowing smoke of the firepit below hurts her eyes. Benjamin follows her out slowly. 'Good work on the house,' he says, putting an arm around her shoulder. 'You did a great job organizing as always.' She can feel him inhale deeply beside her. 'How was the drive down?' she asks. Benjamin starts fiddling with his bowtie. 'Sorry we were late. Declan took the scenic route. Did you enjoy your night out with the girls?' The girls – a group of women she had known since school – didn't get together as much as she would have liked but she still enjoyed their Christmas drinks. 'You could have invited them to this. I mean the house is huge . . .' Benjamin says. 'Oh no,' says Abigail. 'It's nice just to have the same group here. Though, Barbara . . . I hope she's okay. I mean I hope she won't feel like the odd one out.' 'You don't have to worry about Barbara,' says Benjamin. 'I'll watch out for her.' They go back inside, and Abigail closes the balcony door behind them.

Margaret appears then in the doorway wearing a floor-length beaded gown. Her red hair is pinned up and finished with a headband. She looks beautiful. Abigail tries to catch Benjamin's reaction, but he is turned away from her. 'I thought I'd go all out,' says Margaret with a twirl. 'You look lovely,' says Abigail. 'Hey, hey, hey.' Cormac interrupts them. 'I hope there's no collusion going on. I feel like I have a real chance to win this year.' 'No collusion needed,' says Margaret. 'As reigning champion, I look forward to defending my crown.' Declan has arrived at the bedroom door. He has made the bare minimum of effort – he is still wearing his runners and hasn't bothered with a tie. 'It's officially evening time and I still haven't had an alcoholic beverage,' he exclaims. 'This is outrageous. Who do I complain to?' He puts an arm around

Benjamin and propels him out of the room. Margaret rolls her eyes.

Soon everyone is downstairs, dressed to the nines and already in high spirits. Cormac and Stephen are both wearing sharp suits while Olivia and Barbara have played it a little safe with modern cocktail dresses. Abigail puts the last of her bits and pieces in the oven to warm up while Declan pops the first champagne cork.

The evening starts to flow. They drift through the ground floor of the house, eating canapés and topping up drinks. There is music playing: jazz, of course, for the early part of the evening. Barbara, though a little quiet, is now happily talking to Margaret and Benjamin in the corner of the dining room. Abigail, keeping an eye on everything, has to remind herself to relax, though she can never really enjoy herself until after the game has finished. At about ten to eight, Abigail starts handing out the envelopes containing instructions and individual character cards. She instructs them not to open them until the grandfather clock in the hall sounds the hour.

The instructions read:

Welcome everyone and thank you for attending Murder Mystery New Year's Eve 2022!

You should know the situation by now but for anybody new this is how it works: you have each been assigned a specific role to play. This could be a guest, a staff member, a victim, or a detective. I will set the scene: you are in a country mansion in 1929 for a wild New Year's party thrown by Sir Hubert Handesley, who has inherited the estate after the recent death of his father. Some hoped that this would encourage Hubert to grow up, but nothing could be further from the truth. His parties are infamous, and you should expect plenty of champagne, food, good jazz, and some very good gossip. However, in the middle of the evening something terrible will go wrong . . .

In this envelope you will find a character card which gives you information that no one else knows. You will see that there are some specific instructions, but you should feel comfortable to go off-script and do whatever you think your character would do.

You will have some time now to read over this but remember to be careful about the information you share with other people. You don't want anyone beating you to the punch!

Any questions, ask Abigail. She is the narrator for the evening and while she won't be directly involved in solving the crime, she can help you out if you are really stuck.

Abigail eats some canapés, dances a little, sings along to the music and chats with everyone. But she is keeping one eye on the time: she doesn't want it to get too late to start the game. People need to be on the right side of drunk for it to go well. Eventually, she catches Stephen's eye and with a little nod from her they both slip out of the dining room. She is feeling a little giddy, which she puts down to the champagne.

A few minutes later, Abigail emits a high-pitched scream. In the dining room, Margaret nearly drops her glass. Barbara jumps. Declan yells out and grabs his chest. They all laugh once they realize that of course the game has begun. They follow the noise to the kitchen where they discover Stephen lying on the floor with a flowing red scarf below his head. Abigail is standing over him, a hand to her mouth. 'Oh my god!' she says dramatically. 'I just came in here to get myself a glass of water and I came upon this terrible scene: Sir Hubert Handesley dead on the floor, covered in blood. It's just awful. It seems as though someone must have hit him over the head with something. Who could possibly have done this?' Everyone excitedly gathers around the still form of Stephen. 'And we're off,' declares Cormac. He and Margaret immediately start to examine the body. 'I'm not sure if I liked him anyway,' says Benjamin, playfully kicking Stephen's leg. 'Oh, don't out yourself like that,' says Cormac. 'It's too early for the murderer to be revealed.'

Declan stays standing in the doorway. Declan has never guessed who the murderer is. He suspects the whole thing is rigged against him. Abigail has, in past years, purposely given him the least interesting character for this very reason. Last time, she made him the victim, thinking that this would solve the problem, but once the victim became the detective the whole thing fell apart, and Abigail had to take over as the detective instead. This year Declan is the housekeeper. 'You should all inspect the body. See his dishevelled hair,' says Abigail. 'I think he might have put up a fight.' 'There must be a murder weapon nearby,' says Cormac. 'We have to go and find clues now,' Margaret says to Barbara. 'This is the fun part.' Abigail has purposely written a good character for Barbara so that she can become more involved and has given her a lot of juicy clues in her character card. 'Is that something in his coat pocket?' Abigail asks, all wide-eyed and innocent.

Cormac leans over. 'I'll do the honours,' he says as he retrieves the piece of paper. 'It's a letter . . . oh, a racy love letter to the now dearly departed Hubert Handesley from Marjorie Wilde, asking him to run away with her. Who is this Marjorie Wilde?' Olivia squeaks and then puts a hand to her mouth. 'Goddamn you woman,' says Cormac. 'With my own friend?' Olivia pretends to act scandalized. 'I don't think I really want to run away with him . . .' 'Ah, now keep all your clues to yourself,' Abigail says. 'You don't want someone getting help from the secret information you possess on your card.'

It is time then for Stephen to perform his transformation into the Great Detective. He goes into the hallway, removing the blood-red scarf, and dons his deerstalker. Then he re-emerges in the kitchen with a flourish. 'I am Detective Allen. I am sure that you have all heard of me,' he reads from his card. 'I am of course the world's most famous detective. You might be wondering why I am at this party. Well, that's the odd thing! Last week I received a phone call from Sir Hubert saying that an attempt had been made on his life. He thought he was in danger and so he asked me to travel down here to see what could be going on. Never did I imagine that he would be murdered in his own house at his own party! I believe that it is now my duty to solve this crime. None of you can leave until my work is complete. Because one of you must be the murderer. Now, let us have a closer look at this crime scene and see what clues we can find.' Stephen walks around the patch of flagstone he had been lying on just moments ago. He throws the red scarf on the floor to indicate the dead body. 'Well,' says Stephen. 'I'm not sure if this will be pertinent to my investigations, but I think this is the most beautiful dead body I have ever seen in my life.' 'Oh really?' says Cormac, stepping in next to him and frowning theatrically at the scarf. 'You don't think the eyes are a little too close together?' 'I think that the face is proportioned perfectly. Now, what is this . . . ah, it seems that this poor beautiful Adonis has been knocked on the head with something. Has anyone found the murder weapon yet?' Cormac whips around. The hunt is on! Olivia starts searching the kitchen. Barbara is opening cupboards and Declan is scrolling through his phone and sipping his drink. Margaret quickly finds the murder weapon in one of Abigail's favourite hiding places: underneath the sink. She holds the champagne bottle aloft like a trophy. 'Aha!' she says. 'Give me a look, give me a look,' says Cormac. They both examine it carefully. 'Ah yes!' says Stephen. 'This must have been used to hit that poor beautiful man over the head.'

Abigail has given Olivia an important clue about the champagne bottle. She is the only person who knows exactly what everyone was drinking that night and only four of them were drinking champagne. The fingerprints would indicate to the more eagle-eyed amongst them that the murderer was left-handed, further narrowing down the field.

There is only one other clue in the kitchen, and it is Barbara who finds it. She bends down to retrieve the ticket stub which was lodged under the table leg by Abigail just moments previously. 'I'm not sure . . .' she says. 'Is this a clue?' Stephen takes it from her and examines it. 'It must have fallen out of the killer's pocket during the struggle,' he says. He holds it out in front of everyone: a single ticket stub for a production of *An Inspector Calls* from the twenty-third of December.

Everyone scrambles for their character cards to see if they

were present at the theatre. Abigail sees Cormac's eyes light up as he reads from his card that he had witnessed various people in attendance at the play. Already, he has narrowed his field of suspects down to three. Benjamin is being a little quiet, but Abigail knows why: he is the murderer. She changes the victim and the murderer every year, and some people have better poker faces than others. 'You might try and search the rest of the house,' hints Abigail. 'You might even have some luck upstairs.' Everyone dashes off except for Declan, who is still standing glumly near the door to the dining room. 'How long is this going to take, Ab?' he asks. 'Oh, get into the spirit of things,' Abigail says. She hates when he calls her Ab. 'You never know. You might catch the murderer.' 'Not likely,' he mutters.

Occasionally, Abigail will point someone in the right direction if they need it or to keep the game tipping along. She points Barbara towards the pocket watch hidden behind the clock in the sitting room and Barbara is congratulated by everyone on her discovery. On the back of the watch, Abigail has taped an inscription that says simply, *My love, R.* 'You again,' Cormac says to Olivia. Olivia checks her card. 'No, it says here that my initials are MW. It can't be me.' Cormac turns then to Stephen. 'God, you certainly manage to get around,' he says. 'Oh, I'm bad with names, can someone tell me who has the initial R?' 'I'm Angela North,' says Barbara, 'so it's definitely not me.' They all turn to Margaret then. 'A lady never tells,' she replies. 'You absolute minx!' Cormac says with a laugh.

It takes them about two hours in total to find all the clues and red herrings between topping up their drinks and acting out dramatic scenes in Jazz Age voices. Once they have all the clues gathered, they lay them out on the dining room table. 'Very interesting, very interesting,' says Stephen as he surveys them. 'We should gather in the drawing room so that Detective Allen can interrogate us all,' says Abigail.

In the living room, Stephen curls his fake moustache. 'This has been an intriguing case,' he says. 'I have had to use every one of my little grey cells. But still, I need to clarify a number of matters.' He retrieves an envelope from his inside pocket and proceeds with a flourish. 'I will ask each of you a series of questions which you need to answer honestly and openly,' says Stephen, now with a pipe in his mouth. He begins his interrogation: Are you right-handed or left-handed? Do you know of any reason anyone here would have wanted Sir Hubert Handesley dead? Do you speak fluent French? Everyone makes a guess – Margaret guesses Cormac and Cormac guesses Margaret – but none are correct. Abigail has outwitted them this year. 'And finally,' Stephen says, 'will the real killer make themselves known?' Benjamin steps forward. 'I should have known,' wails Stephen. 'My very own best friend.'

*

Around 11 p.m. some fireworks start going off and everyone goes outside but they are too far away to see and there are too many trees blocking the view. Without the light show, they are just disappointing sounds. Abigail is keeping a steady eye on Margaret and her brother, but they are not giving anything away. Very quickly the joys of standing outside in the cold just listening to fireworks wear off and they head back inside, where it is warm.

In the sitting room, Olivia is lounging comfortably in an armchair by herself. 'I've just come to say hello,' says Abigail. 'Oh, that's nice. You don't have to worry though. I'm having a good time,' she says. 'I enjoyed the murder mystery. I think I've got the hang of it now. I'll be in competition next year.' 'I don't know if Cormac would be very pleased if you beat him,' says Abigail. Olivia laughs. 'Yes, I beat him at tennis once – a total fluke but don't tell him that – and we just never spoke about it again.' They both laugh. 'You know I'm plenty competitive too,' Olivia says with a shrug. 'I like to put in the effort. I like to win. But if I don't win, it's not going to ruin my week.' 'That sounds like a very healthy attitude,' says Abigail. Olivia looks up at her. 'It seems silly that we don't know each other that well. I don't know if it's age or what, but I've found it difficult to make friends since I moved here.' 'Oh,' says Abigail. 'Well, we should do something then. With Cormac as well. Or without him.' Olivia looks pleased. 'I keep meaning to ask. Barbara . . .' Olivia leaves the rest of the sentence hanging. Abigail looks to where Barbara is standing near the sitting room door, talking animatedly to someone just out of sight, and then looks back at Olivia. 'Barbara . . .' Olivia continues. 'Cormac and I were wondering. Are she and Benjamin . . . ?' 'Oh,' says Abigail, realizing what the question is. 'Oh no. She's just a work friend.' Olivia doesn't look very convinced. 'Have you met her before?' she asks politely. 'I've met her once or twice before I think. I don't really know her if that's what you mean.' 'No, no I just . . . Cormac was wondering. We didn't know who to ask.'

On the approach to midnight Declan is suddenly spending a lot of time hovering around Barbara *accidentally* placing a hand on her lower back. But Barbara isn't any sort of a push-over. She has had a lot of experience fending off Declans over the years and she'd get away from this one easily enough. Anyway, he is so drunk that when midnight comes, he has forgotten about Barbara and tries to kiss Stephen instead. More champagne bottles are emptied, most of the food has been eaten and then the countdown starts, and the shouts of Happy New Year soon give way to everyone singing 'Happy Birthday' to Benjamin. Abigail hugs her brother tightly around the waist and reaches up to kiss him on the cheek.

The party continues. They dance through the downstairs rooms of the house and out into the courtyard. Declan howls into the night and for once no one is annoyed. Abigail suddenly remembers the cake. She retrieves it from the cupboard, unboxes it and prepares the candles. She peeks her head out the sliding door. Stephen, Margaret and Cormac are outside smoking. 'We're doing the cake now,' Abigail says, 'in the dining room. Where's Benjamin?' But they don't know. The others are in the living room, and she hurries them into the dining room too. 'Where's Benjamin?' she asks Declan as he passes her in the doorway. He shrugs. 'Maybe he's outside,' he says. 'God,' she says. 'The one time I need him, and he goes missing.' 'Maybe he went to the bathroom,' suggests Cormac.

Abigail runs upstairs. The door of the bathroom is ajar, and she pushes against it. But Benjamin isn't there. She lets out a small, frustrated noise and then turns and heads down the corridor towards the master bedroom. She collides with Benjamin as he is exiting the room. 'What are you doing?' she asks. 'Nothing,' he replies. 'Well, we're doing the cake now. In the dining room.' He is a little lethargic and she has to hurry him on with her hands. 'You can't be sleepy already,' she says.

Back downstairs, Margaret turns off the main light and then indicates to Abigail that they are ready for her. Once they see the light of the candles, they all begin to once again sing 'Happy Birthday'. Stephen pushes Benjamin forward and Abigail places the cake in front of him. Once they are finished singing, Abigail puts an arm around him and says, 'Make a wish! Make a wish!' Benjamin leans forward, pausing for just a fraction, and then blows all the candles out in one go. They all cheer and Benjamin blushes. He has become a little shy. Margaret turns on the lights and then they dole out slices of cake, though no one has the appetite. It is no real harm; they will have it for breakfast instead.

Only a half hour later, after tiring himself out, Declan has fallen asleep in the living room. They close the door behind him and continue the party in the rest of the house. Soon Olivia and Cormac decide to go to bed and those left – Benjamin, Stephen, Margaret, Abigail and Barbara – sit down on the floor of the sitting room playing snap and Cluedo and eating the remains of the cheeseboard. They talk about things the way you do in muffled light and champagne-sleepiness. Benjamin's head is resting on the edge of the sofa. Abigail is sitting opposite him. Stephen wants to play Operation and even though they are far too drunk to play it properly they find themselves laughing uproariously at every buzz of the machine. Barbara decides to retire to bed around two.

'Do you remember that time we went camping in your back garden?' Stephen says. 'And just before we were heading out your mother told us casually that there was an escaped prisoner on the loose.' Both Abigail and Benjamin start laughing. 'One of her classics,' says Benjamin. 'You were a very impressionable twelve-year-old.' 'I didn't believe her at first, of course. Thought it was a joke. But then we were telling scary stories, and my imagination went wild,' continues Stephen, 'and a little while after midnight, there was the sound of footsteps outside the tent and a scratching on the canvas . . .' 'And you ran to the back door, but it was locked . . .' says Benjamin. 'You were pounding on it like a maniac.' 'You were so weirdly calm. I thought I was going insane,' says Stephen. 'I was just used to my mother's pranks,' Benjamin replies. 'Mom loved that sort of thing,' says Abigail. 'Totally mad.' 'Anytime you talk about her, it makes me sorry I never met her,' says Margaret. 'You'd have loved her,' says Benjamin. 'She was . . . really funny, a great comedienne. She would do pratfalls to make us laugh. It's weird how she ended up with Dad, but I suppose they balanced each other out.' 'She sang in a choir. She was a great baker. And she always carried red lipstick in her handbag in case she got invited to a party,' says Abigail. 'Oh, that's so lovely,' says Margaret. 'Abigail looks exactly like her now,' says Benjamin. She looks over at him and his eyes are glistening.

Soon, Margaret decides that the night is over for her, and she bids goodnight to the other three. She bends down and kisses Abigail on the cheek and Abigail feels that in this low light, Margaret's eyes are telling her something. She lingers just a little too long at the door.

The final three sit cross-legged on the Persian rug. Their energy levels wane as they talk about school and summer holidays and nightclubs and trips to the Gaeltacht and the house

Stephen and Benjamin rented in the summer after their first year of college.

'Remember when we found that duckling under Dad's car?' Benjamin says to Abigail suddenly. Abigail shakes her head and Benjamin sits up a little straighter. 'You must remember. Dad had gone outside to put the bins out and he heard this tiny quack and there was this duckling under his car near the back wheel.' 'What age was I?' 'Well, I was probably seven, so you were maybe four . . . just turned four . . .' 'I don't remember,' says Abigail. 'Really? I went to collect little insects and worms for him to snack on and you stood guard in case a stray cat found him.' Abigail shakes her head. 'Dad phoned someone,' Benjamin continues, 'who gave him some advice on what to do and . . . I'm not sure what happened then.' 'I don't remember any of that,' says Abigail. 'God, that's so funny. I thought you would have. I forget how small you were.' Benjamin sinks back against the sofa again. 'I suppose we should do our New Year's resolutions,' says Stephen. 'I'm going to do the marathon. I know I've been threatening it for years, but I think now it's really going to happen. And giving up smoking . . .' 'Haven't you been saying you were going to give up smoking every New Year's for the past ten years?' Benjamin says. 'Yes, but pairing it with the marathon will give me the best chance of success,' said Stephen. 'What about you?' he asks Benjamin. 'Oh, I don't know,' Benjamin says. 'I'm not really one for resolutions.' 'And Abigail?' Stephen turns to her. She tells him that she doesn't do resolutions either but that's not the truth. She's just too embarrassed to reveal what they are. They turn back to talking about times when they were teenagers – the teachers they remember, getting drunk for the first time, a girl Benjamin and Stephen nearly fell out over. Abigail mainly just listens, her head resting on the arm of the sofa behind her.

Benjamin decides it is time for bed. Stephen waves at him from the floor but Abigail pulls herself up and hugs and kisses him on each cheek. 'See you in the morning,' she says. Stephen and Abigail whisper-sing 'Happy Birthday' to him as he leaves and there is a final flash of his eyes as the door closes behind him. Stephen yawns but Abigail suddenly feels wide awake. 'I might just do some tidying,' says Abigail, knowing that Stephen will feel obligated to stay and help. They check on Declan, who is snoring. They start gathering all the wine, champagne and beer bottles into one corner and then barrel everything else into rubbish bags. Outside, the fire is silently smouldering. Abigail tosses a saucepan of water over the smoking embers and begins to collect up any rubbish. 'Oh, leave that,' says Stephen. 'I will,' Abigail says but she continues to gather up the rubbish anyway. 'No, I'll do it in the morning. Or you know . . . when we wake up . . .' 'I just want to gather them together to make it easier. Could you get a small bag for the cigarette butts?' Abigail asks. 'No, Abigail, just leave it. Just leave it, please. You're making me feel bad.' He grabs her hands to stop her, and the beer can she is holding falls to the ground. She looks up at him. 'You're so cold,' he says. 'I'll have to warm you up.' He takes off his suit jacket and pulls it across her shoulders. Then, he holds her frozen hands in his and rubs them. He pulls her in closer to him and wraps himself around her so that her body is pressed against his shirted chest. She can feel the warmth of his body. Then his hands are on her shoulders. Then they are in her hair. Suddenly, Abigail doesn't feel cold anymore. She tilts her head back a little and in one motion they both move forward and kiss gently and easily as if they have always done it. Everything around them becomes a void and all she knows are his lips and fingertips. 'Just leave this here. I'll do it in the morning,' says Stephen quietly and Abigail relents. He pushes her inside and then up the staircase. She pauses at the turn of the stair to see him checking that the front door is locked and then going into the living room, presumably to check on Declan. She hesitates a little, wondering what to do, wondering whether to wait but she doesn't want to ruin anything.

Upstairs, Abigail collapses onto her bed. She thinks she could sleep so easily now but first she has to remove her contact lenses and wash her face. The sleepy feeling follows her to the bathroom as she removes her make-up. Back in her bedroom, she takes off her dress and clambers under the duvet. She doesn't remember anything else.

Soon, everyone is asleep. The house is recovering after its upheaval – cigarette butts hidden in the gravel, drops of wine starting to stain the breakfast bar, snores from the living room, the ace of hearts underneath a sofa.

*

Some time on the approach to dawn, Abigail's alarm goes off. She is groggy but she turns on the small bedside lamp, yawns, rubs her face and then gets out of bed. Still in her pyjamas for now, she clears off the table downstairs and moves any bottles to the utility. There must be a bottle bank around here she can drive to later. She starts work on breakfast. She wants everything prepped so that when people start coming downstairs, she can just bung everything in the oven and boil the kettle.

This, for some reason, makes her remember Declan, who of course is not upstairs. She goes to check on him. He is still there, still breathing – she places a hand under his nostrils to be sure. If they're lucky, he might miss breakfast altogether. Margaret is the first to come down. She looks remarkably fresh and glad to find Abigail on her own. They chat a little about the previous night while Margaret makes a pot of tea. Olivia and Cormac are the next to wake followed swiftly by Barbara, who has gone all quiet again. Abigail pre-heats the oven while Cormac and Margaret help with plates and cups and toast. Olivia is trying to figure out the coffee machine – she says it's like the one she has at work but with more buttons. Stephen comes down freshly showered. 'Oh good, coffee,' he says. 'Exactly what I need.' There is a brief discussion about waking Declan, but they think better of it. 'Where is the birthday boy?' Benjamin is still asleep. Stephen goes to check on him but returns to say that there was no answer when he knocked on the door. 'We should let him lie in,' Margaret says, and the others agree. When they are halfway through breakfast, Declan finally comes in. He looks terrible despite his long sleep. Benjamin has still not come downstairs so Stephen says he will try him again. 'I'll drag him out of the bed if I have to,' he says. 'He's had enough of a lie-in.' But he soon returns to say that the bedroom door is locked. Abigail goes back upstairs with him. They knock at the door loudly and call his name but there is no response. And the door is indeed locked. They call his phone. They can hear it ringing but it goes to voicemail without waking him. 'Hi, it's Ben here . . .' Abigail doesn't like it when he calls himself Ben. That's not his name. That's what other people call him. It's not right. Margaret has now joined them, and she can see that they are worried. 'We need to break down the door,' Stephen says. This is easier said than done. The banging brings the others upstairs. Cormac has a go, but the door doesn't budge. Suddenly Declan is there. He throws himself at the door and it crashes open. He nearly falls into the room. Abigail pushes past the others. Stephen is just behind. She calls out Benjamin's name. But something isn't right. He isn't quite himself. She puts a hand to his chest, and he is cold.

PART TWO

'He read all night from sundown to dawn, and all day from sunup to dusk, until with virtually no sleep and so much reading he dried out his brain and lost his sanity . . . He decided to turn himself into a knight errant, travelling all over the world with his horse and his weapons, seeking adventures and doing everything that, according to his books, earlier knights had done.'

Don Quixote, MIGUEL DE CERVANTES

'Every murderer is probably somebody's old friend.'

The Mysterious Affair at Styles, AGATHA CHRISTIE

CAST OF CHARACTERS
(IN ORDER OF APPEARANCE)

Auguste Bell is our esteemed detective. Previously seen in the international bestsellers *The Guilty Vicarage* and *The Fountain Pen Mystery*, he will solve this case in fewer than thirty chapters. He is a little bit Poirot, a smidge of Holmes and a surprising amount of Inspector French.

The butler has wanted to be a butler since he was five years old. He reads Tolstoy in the original Russian, is allergic to shellfish and has fired three people for stealing silver.

Margaret is the auburn-haired ex-fiancée of the deceased. She still wears the engagement ring hidden on a chain around her neck.

The doctor thinks he has already solved it.

The local police inspector wants an easy life.

Abigail is the sister of the deceased.

Stephen is a schoolfriend of the deceased. He knows he is attractive and uses it to his advantage. Always thinks he is the lead character in everything.

Declan is a childhood friend of the deceased. He likes greyhound racing and penalty tries.

Barbara is the secretary of the deceased, but then who invites their secretary to New Year's?

Cormac is a university friend of the deceased. He doesn't like to lose. Olivia is the most important thing in his life.

Olivia is Cormac's fiancée. She was a champion gymnast in her youth and as a teenager she ran away and lived with circus-folk for the summer before her foster parents found her and brought her home.

Dorcas the maid has worked for the family for nearly thirty years. She is both incredibly loyal and an inveterate gossip.

Detective Inspector Ferret is the policeman.

Sacker is a Watson. To quote A. A. Milne's introduction to the 1926 edition of *The Red House Mystery*: 'Are we to have a Watson? We are . . . A little slow, let him be, as many of us are, but friendly, human, likeable . . .'

The aunt is the sister of Abigail's deceased father. Her age is unknown. Many men have left her large sums of money in their wills, much to their wives' chagrin.

The innkeepers are genuinely happy.

The psychic believes everything she says.

Lord and Lady Mallowan, their son Freddie and their daughter Clarissa are the owners of most of the land in the county. They like having power and don't realize how quickly it can disappear.

The gardener is just trying to make a living.

Benjamin is dead.

FAIR PLAY RULES

T. S. Eliot's rules in 'Homage to Wilkie Collins:
An omnibus review of nine mystery novels',
published in *New Criterion* in January 1927:

1. The story must not rely upon elaborate and incredible
   disguises . . . Disguises must be only occasional and
   incidental.
2. The character and motives of the criminal should be
   normal.
3. The story must not rely either upon occult phenomena,
   or, what comes to the same thing, upon mysterious and
   preposterous discoveries made by lonely scientists.
4. Elaborate and bizarre machinery is an irrelevance . . .
   Writers who delight in treasures hid in strange places,
   cyphers and codes, runes and rituals, should not be
   encouraged.
5. The detective should be highly intelligent but not
   superhuman. We should be able to follow his inferences
   and almost, but not quite, make them with him.

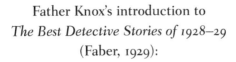

Father Knox's introduction to
The Best Detective Stories of 1928–29
(Faber, 1929):

1. The criminal must be someone mentioned in the early part of the story, but must not be anyone whose thoughts the reader has been allowed to follow.
2. All supernatural or preternatural agencies are ruled out as a matter of course.
3. Not more than one secret room or passage is allowable.
4. No hitherto undiscovered poisons may be used, nor any appliance which will need a long scientific explanation at the end.
5. No Chinaman must figure in the story.
6. No accident must ever help the detective, nor must he ever have an unaccountable intuition which proves to be right.
7. The detective must not himself commit the crime.
8. The detective must not light on any clues that are not instantly produced for the inspection of the reader.
9. The stupid friend of the detective, the Watson, must not conceal any thoughts which pass through his mind; his intelligence must be slightly, but very slightly, below that of the average reader . . . he exists for the purpose of letting the reader have a sparring partner, as it were, against whom he can pit his brains. 'I may have been a fool,' he says to himself as he puts the book down, 'but at least I wasn't such a doddering fool as poor old Watson.'
10. Twin brothers, and doubles generally, must not appear unless we have been duly prepared for them.

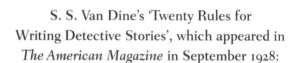

S. S. Van Dine's 'Twenty Rules for Writing Detective Stories', which appeared in *The American Magazine* in September 1928:

1. The reader must have equal opportunity with the detective for solving the mystery.
2. No wilful tricks or deceptions may be played on the reader.
3. There must be no love interest in the story.
4. The detective himself, or one of the official investigators, should never turn out to be the culprit.
5. The culprit must be determined by logical deductions— not by accident or coincidence or unmotivated confession.
6. The detective novel must have a detective in it; and a detective is not a detective unless he detects.
7. There simply must be a corpse in a detective novel, and the deader the corpse the better.
8. The problem of the crime must be solved by strictly naturalistic means.
9. There must be but one detective—that is, but one protagonist of deduction—one *deus ex machina*.
10. The culprit must turn out to be a person who has played a more or less prominent part in the story.
11. Servants—such as butlers, footmen, valets, game-keepers, cooks, and the like—must not be chosen by the author as the culprit.
12. There must be but one culprit, no matter how many murders are committed.
13. Secret societies, camorras, mafias, et al., have no place in a detective story.

14. The method of murder, and the means of detecting it, must be rational and scientific.

15. The truth of the problem must at all times be apparent—provided the reader is shrewd enough to see it.

16. A detective novel should contain no long descriptive passages, no literary dallying with side-issues, no subtly worked-out character analyses, no 'atmospheric' preoccupations.

17. A professional criminal must never be shouldered with the guilt of a crime in a detective story.

18. A crime in a detective story must never turn out to be an accident or a suicide.

19. The motives for all crimes in detective stories should be personal.

20. And (to give my Credo an even score of items) I herewith list a few of the devices which no self-respecting detective-story writer will now avail himself of . . . Determining the identity of the culprit by comparing the butt of a cigarette left at the scene of the crime with the brand smoked by a suspect. The bogus spiritualistic séance to frighten the culprit into giving himself away. Forged fingerprints. The dummy-figure alibi. The dog that does not bark and thereby reveals the fact that the intruder is familiar. The final pinning of the crime on a twin, or a relative who looks exactly like the suspected, but innocent, person. The hypodermic syringe and the knockout drops. The commission of the murder in a locked room after the police have actually broken in. The word-association test for guilt. The cipher, or code letter, which is eventually unravelled by the sleuth.

Chapter One

THE DETECTIVE ARRIVES

The case that made Auguste Bell famous was not his most difficult nor his most spectacular but it *was* his most important. Though he had achieved so much in his career since then, he would always prize that first case above all others.

His whole future had changed that day on the ferry boat from Tallinn on his way to see his old friend Sven Hjerson. A dead body was discovered on board and within two hours, Bell had investigated the crime, interrogated witnesses, performed a citizen's arrest and fully explained the solution to the stunned police waiting at the ferry port in Helsinki.

The press had dubbed it *The Mysterious Affair of the Ferry Crossing*, though Bell hadn't found the matter very mysterious at all. In fact, the solution was straightforward: the body discovered was not that of Lady Frankenthorpe's travelling companion, but was in fact the heiress to the Frankenthorpe cat food empire herself. The companion – a poor distant cousin – had been having an affair with a leading member of an Estonian criminal gang who had been looking for a quick escape from his tough crime-ridden life. They had together planned to fake the wealthy woman's death and then, with the aid of wigs and make-up, have the companion take the place of the heiress who was to come into her fortune the following month when she turned twenty-five. The couple would then cash out and run away together.

The clues were myriad: the soft pampered hands of the deceased, the fact that the apparent heiress had gained weight seemingly overnight and an intriguing event that had been recounted to Bell only a few nights before at a dinner party in Tallinn. A guest at the dinner had met Lady Frankenthorpe a few weeks prior at a hotel in Vilnius and had remarked, with barely contained disdain, that the woman had ordered her scrambled eggs well done. In the aftermath of the murder and knowing full well that no true European heiress would ever eat dry eggs, Bell realized that this hotel breakfast must have been a trial run for the companion and her criminal lover and with the aid of other clues he quickly deduced what had happened.

The ferry security made sure that the fake heiress was unable to escape, and sure enough her poor man was waiting for her in handcuffs at the port. Bell became the toast of the town, and many socialites and members of the aristocracy invited him to their country mansions or Caribbean resorts in the hope that some thrilling murder might take place. And quite often it did – a fact that disturbed him only slightly.

And so began his life as a consulting detective. He continued to solve cases, and his reputation grew.

*

As the driver parked the Daimler limousine in the already crowded turning circle of the grand house that lay in front of him, Bell noticed that next to the flash cars were the more sombre sights of an ambulance and police vehicle.

To the average observer, it may have seemed as though Auguste Bell did nothing more than walk from the motor-car to the front door of the house. But anyone who knew the detective would tell you that he had already made half a dozen observations on that short journey. The Daimler retreated down the impressive driveway as the front door was duly answered by a man Bell took to be the butler. Bell introduced himself and was invited inside but before the butler could even take Bell's overcoat, a red-headed young woman appeared.

'Ah, there you are,' she said. She looked a little frazzled, but her steely eyes belied an inner strength. She introduced herself as Margaret and ushered him towards the drawing room.

'We're in here,' she said, but Bell didn't follow her.

'Hold on, mademoiselle,' he said, handing his coat, gloves, hat, and scarf to the butler. 'I have two questions I need answered first.' He coughed lightly. 'First, did it rain any time during the night?'

Margaret blinked.

'I don't— I don't recall,' she said.

'Of course not,' Bell replied. 'And my second question is, does this house have gas central heating?'

Margaret looked at him, startled by the inanity of the question.

'I think so,' she said. 'But I don't see—'

'Ah! That is fine. I will go upstairs now to inspect the crime scene and speak with the police and the doctor.'

Margaret looked faintly annoyed.

'Won't you come to the drawing room first?' she said. 'Even just to meet Abigail?'

'No, I'm afraid not just yet. You must excuse me. It is,' Bell clarified, 'my method.' He headed for the stairs before she could say anything else, and soon he heard the door of the drawing room close behind her.

As Bell ascended the stairs, he took note of every creak of a floorboard, every imperfection in the polished banisters and papered walls. He checked that the lights were working. He admired the beautiful stained-glass window. He inspected the collection of shotguns and other hunting weapons mounted on the wall of the landing, noting the blank space in the centre. He noticed a spot of damp on the ceiling above him. A dried leaf, probably brought inside on the bottom of someone's shoe, was stuck to the carpet.

All this information would gently stew in his brain until eventually – around about Chapter Twenty-Three – the solution would come bubbling to the surface.

He did not need to be told the room in which the tragedy had occurred: it was obvious.

Chapter Two

THE EVIDENCE OF THE DOCTOR

In the bedroom, there was one doctor, one young police officer and one dead body. Bell took in everything in an instant.

'I am Auguste Bell, the consulting detective. You may have heard of me,' he said, handing the doctor his business card. 'I have been contacted by the lady of the house to investigate her brother's death.' The doctor glanced at the card and then eyed Bell suspiciously.

'She's wasting your time,' the doctor said.

'What do you mean?' asked Bell curiously.

'It's a suicide. Clear and simple.'

'There is no doubt at all in your mind?' Bell enquired.

'Absolutely none.'

'The deceased's sister seemed quite certain in my phone call with her that this was not a—'

The doctor sighed deeply. 'Family are always convinced that it couldn't possibly be suicide. They don't want to believe it. They want to be told that it was an aneurysm, a heart attack, a stroke –' the doctor gestured towards Bell – 'a murder – unfortunately, things are what they are. I look at the facts of the situation, the science, that is my job.'

'It is correct that you have a job to do,' said Bell. 'But I have a job to do as well.'

The doctor shrugged and snapped his case shut.

'Could you answer a few questions before you—?' asked Bell.

The doctor interrupted him. 'I know the routine by now, Bell,' he said. 'The time of death was somewhere between three and four a.m. The method of death – well, I will of course have a more accurate idea once I perform the autopsy. The door was locked from the inside and had to be broken down by the house guests. All in all, an open and shut case. I hope you won't charge that poor lady too much.'

*

It was time now to move the body out to the waiting ambulance. Bell moved to the side in order to allow the paramedics to do their job. As they lifted the body from the bed onto the stretcher, Bell noticed something shiny falling gently out of the dead man's pyjama pocket and become hidden in the folds of the duvet beneath. Bell glanced at the faces of the others in the room but realized that none of them had seen what he had spotted. Once the doctor and paramedics had left, Bell discreetly moved towards the bed and pocketed the small object.

He did not have any time to inspect it, however, as he was swiftly joined at the murder scene by the local police inspector. He didn't look too happy, Bell thought, though of course it was New Year's Day, and the inspector had probably been looking forward to an uneventful shift. He was a tall thin man with a moustache and an air of superiority about him. He eyed Bell warily.

Bell started to introduce himself, but the inspector stopped him.

'I know who you are,' he said. 'They told me you were coming. I'm afraid it will have been a wasted trip.'

'Ah! So, you agree with the assessment made by the good doctor?' asked Bell.

'It's a suicide. An easy case, thank god,' the inspector said. Bell politely ignored him.

'You might permit me to ask you a few questions anyway. I will of course be very grateful for any assistance,' Bell said.

'Of course,' said the inspector. 'I always like to help out a fellow professional.' He smirked. Bell got the impression that the police inspector did not have much time for consulting detectives like himself.

'Has anything been moved? Has anything been disarranged in the room?' Bell asked him.

'Of course not,' the inspector said. 'My men are highly trained professionals. They know not to touch anything.'

'Yes, but once the doctor declared it a suicide – I know that sometimes it is easy to take one's eye off the ball,' said Bell.

But the inspector shook his head sternly. 'Not here sir, not today. Not under my watch.'

'This door to the balcony, it was open when you arrived?' asked Bell.

'The door was unlocked but closed. One of my men then went outside to inspect the balcony but that was all.'

'And the alarm clock was like this on the floor?'

'One of my officers brought that to my attention when I arrived. This clock has not been moved. Its face was smashed just like this. You will see that the clock has stopped, and the time shows half past three, which is when the doctor says the man died.'

'Yes, very convenient. Well, thank you very much,' said Bell. 'You and your men have done an admirable job here.'

'It is very sad,' said the inspector, suddenly sombre. 'This is not the first suicide I have been called out to investigate in my career. I am sorry for his sister, of course, and the rest of the household. But as the doctor said, we just focus on the facts.'

'You have completed your job,' said Bell, 'and so now I suppose I will start mine.'

Once the room had been cleared, Bell carefully put a hand in his pocket and took out the object he had swiped from the bed: a single gold earring.

Chapter Three

THE EVIDENCE OF THE MURDER SCENE

First, he inspected the door. He checked the locking system, the handles on either side and the hinges. The key had been placed on top of a chest of drawers. He inspected it carefully. There were tiny abrasions along the bit, but it was an old key and so it was impossible to say how long those scratches had been there. He logged a mental note anyway.

He turned and took in the room: it was large and spacious with plenty of natural sunlight. The bed-sheets were crumpled in a heap. On the floor to the left of the bed was the smashed alarm clock. Half past three. He wondered.

There were two windows in the room: he examined both of them and found that they were secure, there was no broken glass on the sill or floor underneath the windows and they were both shut tight from the inside. He then turned his attention to the large double glass doors leading to the balcony. He found that they had not been tampered with – no damage to the hinges or bolt – but of course the door had been unlocked when the police arrived. It was a cold winter's day and so it seemed unlikely that the deceased would have spent much time outside.

He went out onto the balcony, which was empty except for two objects: a deflated football and a broken bird feeder. The surface of the balcony hadn't been maintained very well and was a little slippery underfoot. He examined the cast-iron railings and found that they were sturdy.

From the balcony he had a bird's eye view of the patio at the back of the house. He could see a fire with cooled embers, some empty bottles of alcohol and a small collection of cigarette butts. And directly below, in a plant pot, a champagne bottle lay on its side. *It must have been some party*, Bell thought to himself. He wondered how easy it would be to climb onto the balcony from below. There was a trellis which might make the job relatively straightforward for an athletic person. He would need to conduct an experiment later, he thought. It reminded him of a previous case of his, *The Triple Petunia Murder*, but plots tended not to repeat themselves, in his experience.

Back inside, he checked the en suite: there was a bottle of shampoo and some soap in the shower, there was a toothbrush, some toothpaste, and a razor by the sink. No pills or medications. Nothing of note.

In the chest of drawers there were clothes and underthings. In the wardrobe, there were fine suits, shooting outfits and large coats.

In the drawer of the nightstand there was a nice watch – which hadn't been broken and was showing the correct time – and some reading glasses. Next to the lamp was an empty bottle of sleeping pills.

He was finished with his inspection.

He went downstairs where the household awaited him in the drawing room.

'I am sorry for not coming in first to introduce myself,' Bell said, 'but each detective has his own methods. I prefer to examine the crime scene first without any interference – whether that be physical or psychological. I have now done that and so I am ready to speak to each of you in turn and answer any initial questions you might have.'

The group stared up at him, each individual pale and frightened. Bell studied their faces carefully. No one knew what to say.

'Maybe we could start with the introductions,' he proposed.

A young woman with dark hair and clear blue eyes stood up and said hesitantly, 'I am Abigail. We spoke on the phone.'

'Oh, yes, of course. Abigail.' Bell leaned across and shook her hand. 'My sincere condolences to you on the loss of your dear brother,' he said.

'This is Stephen,' she said, turning to the man sitting next to her. Stephen stood to shake Bell's hand. He was an attractive man with light brown hair.

'Stephen went to school with Benjamin. They've known each other a long time,' said Abigail.

'Over twenty years,' said Stephen. He was stony-faced.

'This has been such a shock for you, I'm sure,' said Bell.

A larger man, ruddy-cheeked, stinking of alcohol and dressed in a rumpled suit, declared himself to be Declan.

'A good friend of Benj. Known him since we were five years old.'

Bell duly shook his hand. He had already met Margaret, of course, and next to her was a woman who introduced herself as Barbara.

'Did you also go to school with Mr—?' Bell started to ask.

'No, I work— I'm his secretary,' she explained. Bell took note of the hesitation in her voice. He also noticed a nearly imperceptible distance between her and the others. This was something he would have to tease out over the coming chapters.

Finally, the young couple. The man introduced himself as Cormac and his fiancée as Olivia.

'Fiancée?' uttered Margaret. Everyone else stared.

'Yes, we were planning to announce it sometime today, but . . .' Cormac didn't need to say anything else. He looked to Olivia, and she clasped her hand in his.

'Congratulations,' whispered Abigail.

'Yes, congratulations,' intoned the others.

'I knew Ben from university,' said Cormac. 'And Olivia has known him now for a couple of years.'

'You are all good friends it seems. It is important to have friends you can remain close to in times like these. It is a great support,' said Bell.

'You are right, of course. But this morning has been very stressful for all of us. We will need to head home soon,' said Cormac. 'We really have to leave. Olivia – we – we need to be at home. It's the best place for us.'

Abigail stood suddenly.

'You can't go. Not yet,' she said. 'Not until we've solved this.'

'Yes,' said Bell. 'Unfortunately, you will not be permitted to leave until my investigations are complete.'

'And how long will that be?' asked Cormac.

'However long it takes,' said Bell.

'Exactly,' said Abigail.

'Of course,' said Stephen softly, and Margaret nodded.

Cormac looked as though he might argue the point, but Olivia patted his hand gently and he relaxed a little. An odd feeling came over Bell then, a sense that he was being transported back in time, some rustle of a memory that he couldn't grasp hold of quickly enough before it receded.

'I think it would be a good idea to have something to eat,' continued Bell. 'Even if you feel you don't want it, force yourselves. You will need sustenance. You have all suffered a shock and you will need to keep your strength up. And I will first speak to . . . Abigail?'

She lifted her head towards him.

'Is there another room we can use?' the detective asked her, and Abigail silently led him to the library.

GARDAÍ INVESTIGATING 'ALL CIRCUMSTANCES' AFTER MAN'S BODY FOUND IN AIRBNB PROPERTY ON NEW YEAR'S DAY

Sun Jan 01, 2023 – 13:24

A garda investigation is under way after the body of a man in his early 30s was found at a house following a New Year's Eve party.

His body was removed to the morgue at CUH in the last couple of hours. A post-mortem will take place at a later date.

The Gardaí say that the results of the exam will determine the course of their investigation and that they are probing 'all circumstances' surrounding the discovery.

Chapter Four

THE EVIDENCE OF THE SISTER

In the library, Bell settled himself in an armchair opposite Abigail. It was a dark room with rows and rows of books touching the high ceiling. It smelled a little of cigar smoke and whiskey. There was something reassuring about the room, Bell thought.

'I believe this was supposed to be a birthday party—' he started.

'Yes, my brother's birthday is – today.' Abigail closed her eyes. 'God, I'd forgotten about that already,' she said. Bell gave her a moment to collect herself.

She continued, 'And so as we quite often do, we paired a New Year's Eve party with a birthday party. We invited friends down to stay for a couple of days. We've been doing it for years now.' Her voice had become very quiet.

'And is it just you and your brother in the house?'

'Yes, both of our parents are deceased. Our mother died when I was thirteen years old, and our father died about ten years ago. Benjamin is generally away during the week, in the city – he took over the family business, you see, after our father died – but he comes home at weekends.'

'And you—'

'I run the house as best I can, and I volunteer with a local charity in the village.'

'I have a couple of quick questions, the first being – can you tell me a little bit more about your brother's mood in the days coming up to the party?'

'We spent Christmas here together, just the two of us as usual. We sent the servants home. We like the little break. He was in a good mood. He so rarely takes time off. But Christmas is a promise we make to each other. He went back to the city for a few days to finish up a couple of things and then he drove back yesterday. He seemed fine. Happy. Himself. I don't recall anything amiss with him.'

'Did your brother have any enemies?' asked Bell. 'Were there any threats against him? Anybody who would do him harm?'

'No, no. I don't really know what his life in the city is like, but everyone liked Benjamin.'

'Did your brother have any financial difficulties? Any debts?'

'No,' said Abigail. 'We're comfortable.'

'Did your brother ever have difficulty sleeping?'

'Not that I know of. He never told me about any problems.'

'And finally, why do you disagree with the police assessment that this was simply a suicide?'

Abigail took a large breath.

'The police don't know what they are talking about. When they arrived, it was clear that they didn't want to investigate it properly. They had their minds made up,' Abigail said, her voice catching.

'But the evidence of the doctor—?'

'He wasn't here last night, he didn't see— There were no signs, no clues. I know my brother. I would have known. I would have seen. It couldn't—' She broke off then and looked up at Bell again. 'And anyway, it couldn't possibly be a suicide. It would break Van Dine's Eighteenth Commandment.* It wouldn't make any sense.'

Her eyes were bright and pleading.

'I need your help,' she said. 'I need you to help me figure out what happened.'

Bell paused for a moment and stroked his chin. He was contemplating everything he had been told.

'I believe I can help you,' he said calmly. 'In fact, I believe that all the clues I will need are in this house. But first, please recount for me what happened since you awoke yesterday morning.'

Abigail, looking suddenly relieved, talked him through the previous day: the arrivals, the dinner, the drinks, the fireworks and then bed.

'What time did you go to sleep?'

'It was sometime after three. I'm not exactly sure.'

'So, let's see if I have this right: everyone was asleep upstairs except for one person – Declan, who fell asleep in the drawing room.'

'That's correct,' she said. 'Stephen went up to bed just after me.'

'Ah, I see. And was there any animosity between the guests? I mean, did any of them quarrel with your brother?'

Abigail shook her head. 'No,' she said. 'We are all good friends. I mean, Margaret . . . Benjamin and Margaret had

---

* A crime in a detective story must never turn out to be an accident or a suicide.

been engaged some time ago and it was broken off. But they were on good terms. Everyone else is a long-term friend – people we've known for absolutely years. Except Barbara and Olivia, of course.'

'Yes, Olivia – do you know much about her?'

'She has been seeing Cormac for a little over three years now, so we know her well enough but I'm afraid that I'm not close with her. Cormac is Benjamin's friend from university. I only see him once or twice a year. Olivia seems pleasant, though. Benjamin liked her as well. He probably knew her better than I did.'

'And Stephen?'

'Oh well, Benjamin and I have known Stephen since we were young. Stephen is a great friend to both of us.'

'Ah yes, and I understand that Barbara worked at your family's business. Is it usual for Benjamin to invite someone from work to a birthday party?'

Abigail hesitated.

'He'd never done it before,' she said. 'I think he felt a little sorry for her. He said she had no family, and she would be alone – it's the time of year and all that. He had work to do over the New Year and so he invited her to come stay. She types up letters for him.'

'Ah, your brother was a very generous man,' said Bell. 'And then this morning . . . ?' His tone became gentler now. Abigail closed her eyes and recounted everything that had happened that morning from the time that she had woken up.

'Did your brother always lock his room?'

'I never knew him to, but then it is usually just the two of us here.'

'Of course.'

Bell could see tears forming in Abigail's eyes. He tried to distract her. He put his hand in his pocket and took out the earring he had discovered during the moving of the body.

'Ah, I knew there was something. Does this earring perhaps belong to you?' he asked. Abigail took the earring from him and inspected it carefully.

'No,' she said, returning it to him. 'It's not one of mine.'

'Do you recognize it? I mean, have you seen any of the guests wearing this pair of earrings?'

'No, but then I couldn't be sure. I don't notice those kinds of things. They don't seem like Margaret's style, but I can't say for Olivia and Barbara. Sorry I can't be of more help.'

He replaced the earring in his pocket.

'Is it important?' Abigail asked.

'I'm not sure yet,' Bell said. 'It may well be a red herring. We will have to see. I will let you go now. I think it would be a good idea for you to take a little nap. And I would encourage you once more to have something to eat even if you don't feel particularly hungry. Keep your strength up.'

'Do you want to interview the others?' she asked.

'Yes, eventually. Right now, I need to organize my thoughts,' said Bell.

To: Abigail
From: Fred (HR)
Re: compassionate leave
Date: 3 January 2023

Abigail,

I refer to your below email and confirm your upcoming leave for a period of two weeks.

I would like to extend our condolences once again and if you need anything either during your leave or after please do not hesitate to contact me at my email address or direct dial.

As I have previously said, I set out below contact details for bereavement services, including counselling, that are provided free of charge to all employees.

Chapter Five

A LOCKED-ROOM LECTURE

B ell sat in quiet contemplation. He could tell even at this early juncture that this was going to be a tricky case. He felt that Abigail hadn't fully realized the task that she had set for him, and he worried that the solution she sought was unlikely to make her happy.

But still, he had a job to do.

Once he felt ready and refreshed, he rejoined the group in the drawing room where, he was pleased to see, some of them were drinking tea and eating. He was offered a cup and a tuna sandwich by Abigail, but he waved them away.

'Have you figured it out already?' asked Declan.

'No, not even I could solve this crime in such a short amount of time,' said Bell.

'Crime?' asked Cormac. 'So, it is murder?'

'I am a detective. Solving murders is what I do. If this wasn't a murder, I wouldn't be here.'

Stephen put down his plate. He suddenly looked very unwell.

'I hope you won't drag this out,' said Declan.

'I will take only the time needed to solve this matter.'

Bell cleared his throat, and everyone instinctively put down their cups and plates and utensils.

'What we have here,' Bell declared, 'is a locked-door mystery.'

He paused for effect.

'Before we begin properly, for reference purposes only, I would like to ask the reader to turn back a few pages and read through the Fair Play Rules which you probably skipped earlier. I will wait here for your return. My own personal preference is for the Knox Decalogue. Don't be fooled by number five. It is not as problematic as it seems.* You are, I hope,' he continued, 'familiar with Dr Fell's Locked-Room Lecture in Chapter Fifteen of John Dickson Carr's *The Hollow Man*. You might similarly be familiar with the discussion of same in Chapter Thirteen of Clayton Rawson's *Death from a Top Hat* or John Pugmire's excellent article in *Crime and Detective Stories*, number fifty-nine. First, I will need to discover whether the murderer was in the room at the time of the killing or not. This will be the crux of the matter. Second, there are a number of things we can already rule out: I will discount the supernatural for reasons of personal antipathy, though you may disagree –'

He paused here but nobody protested.

'There is no chimney, so that is out. I have searched the room for a mechanical device but could not find any. There is no hidden aperture in the room – I have conducted a thorough examination. No poisonous snakes or the like. I can also say with some confidence that the door hinges and windows

---

* '[Knox was] poking fun at thriller writers whose reliance on sinister Oriental villains had already become a racist cliché' – *The Golden Age of Murder* by Martin Edwards

have not been tampered with. The balcony door has also not been tampered with, though it was unlocked, which provides the possibility of an entrance for the killer.'

'So, what do you think could have happened here?' Margaret asked, getting straight to the point.

'I have only working theories, all of which involve some element of illusion or trickery. They will take some more time to form and rise to the surface of my mind. I will need to interview all the guests and staff – maybe more than once. I will need to examine every inch of this house. I will need to disentangle things. Please forgive me if I come across other revelations in my detection work. It happens sometimes. And I cannot emphasize enough at this point that if my deductions so far are correct, that means that somebody in this house was responsible for Benjamin's death.' He looked slowly around him at each face. 'The murderer is one of you,' he said in sombre tones.

'Is there any chance an outsider was involved? If the balcony door was unlocked . . .' Abigail asked. 'Could someone have come in through the balcony and then escaped?'

Bell looked at her deeply and with great care.

'I will of course investigate all possibilities, but right now I find it unlikely that your brother's death happened in the way you have described.'

He watched her carefully.

'I suppose it seems a little dramatic,' she admitted.

'It is not the dramatics that turn me off the idea, but the logistics. In Chapter Twenty-Two I will conduct an experiment with the help of Cormac, Stephen and a young policeman who will each try to climb to the balcony. They will all fail. But of course, I have come to no conclusions yet. Does anyone have any questions at this juncture?' he asked.

But nobody did.

*

A bigail wanted to be cremated. She had told Benjamin sometime after the death of their father. She had sat through enough funerals now to know exactly what she wanted. She was certain: 'Scatter my ashes on their graves and on the cliffs near the cove.' She thinks he wanted the same, but the memory isn't strong enough and so now, tasked with the decision of what to do with his remains, she isn't quite sure. Her aunt has come with her to meet with the funeral directors. Abigail appreciates the way her aunt had stepped in ably after the death of each parent and she recognizes her importance as a link in a chain going back generations. But she can also be a little traditional. That isn't quite the correct word. A little bit superstitious or something. She isn't a mass-going Catholic, but she prays to St Anthony and had buried a few Children of Prague in her time. She has on occasion visited fortune tellers and even has a special place in her house for her crystal collection. Her aunt is adamant that Benjamin should be buried and is mildly horrified at the thought of cremation. 'He should be buried with your parents. It's what your mother would have wanted,' she says, her voice just a whisper. And so, in the shock of it all, Abigail goes along with it. Her aunt picks out the casket because that's not something Abigail cares about but when she starts talking about prayers and hymns Abigail puts her foot down. No religion. It wouldn't be right. 'Maybe just a blessing from a priest,' her aunt says. 'No, nothing.' Abigail is insistent. 'We will have readings, poetry, eulogies – whatever. But no priests,' she says. The funeral director takes a note. 'But Abigail, I mean, just in case . . .' 'Suicides don't go to heaven according to the Catholic church, so it won't matter either way,' Abigail says, her skin buzzing. She feels winded somehow though she hasn't moved from her chair. There is nothing her aunt can really say. It is a blunt fact. They pick a time and date and talk about the obituary. 'I don't want anything that says *tragically* or *suddenly* or *unexpectedly*,' Abigail says. 'Just *died* will be fine. And mention his friends. List them out. That's important. That was important to him.' She drives her aunt home afterwards and they sit in the car for a while just talking about nothing in particular. Everything in Abigail's life is about organizing at the moment. It's like getting married. Her aunt is telling her about all the people she has phoned or written to let them know. Abigail doesn't really see the point. 'It's important to allow people the opportunity to give their condolences. Not everyone is checking the obituaries regularly. You can miss things and I know there are people who would be very put out if they couldn't come to the removal.' Abigail is not particularly concerned about other people's feelings these days, but she recognizes this for what it is: her aunt's way of handling another tragic loss. She is just not sure that she is up to dealing with everyone, to being outside of her house and having to put on tights and uncomfortable shoes. The routine of death is wearying and seems designed with everyone in mind except her. That evening, she phones Margaret to tell her about the arrangements. Abigail wants people to speak at the funeral. Whatever they want: a remembrance or a poem or a song. Margaret tells her not to worry, that she will organize that side of things. She knew she could depend on Margaret. Abigail only has dead time now to fill before the funeral. She watches episodes of *Friends* one after the other – they slowly fade into the next. She boils the kettle to make pasta and then realizes she isn't hungry. She fills her hot water bottle instead and curls up on the sofa. Another cold open begins. She becomes fixated on the actresses' bodies. She never realized how thin they were before. She is sleepy, and she could fall asleep right here, but she also knows that once she goes upstairs to bed, she will never sleep. Something will happen to make her suddenly uncomfortable and wide awake. She starts crying – there is no reason, no obvious trigger – and tears flow down her cheeks. She is sobbing now. Outside on the roadway, she can hear someone putting out their bins. A car passes by. The title tune starts to play. She goes to the fruit bowl, chooses a banana and eats it. She opens her food cupboard and stands there paralyzed by choice. She sits again but now in a different chair – a dining room chair – that is less comfortable than the sofa. She hugs the hot water bottle to her. She thinks of ways to comfort herself through food or music or sleep, but nothing feels right. Nothing will satiate her. She should wash her hair but then she'd have to undress and the thought of that is completely unbearable. She should go to bed. She turns the television off, switches off the lights, feels her way up the stairs in the dark and falls into her bed, hauling her body under the duvet. Her stomach grumbles. Her pillow is uncomfortable. She lies there for two hours before falling asleep. She wakes suddenly thinking she has heard a noise and when she checks the time, she realizes that she has only been asleep for a handful of minutes. She is confused then and thinks she might have forgotten to turn the house alarm on, but once she reaches halfway down the stairs, she realizes that of course everything is fine: the green light on the security panel is blinking reassuringly. She falls asleep and then wakes and falls asleep and wakes before finally sleeping soundly from just after three until her phone goes off at eight.

Chapter Six

THE EVIDENCE OF THE STAFF

Bell decided that he would conduct his investigations from the library. First, he asked Abigail to tell him about the staff.

'Well, there's Dorcas, our maid, who lives with us during the week and goes back to her little cottage at weekends. We also have a butler, Mr O'Brien, who has been with my family for a long time. We normally have a cook and a kitchen assistant, but they have both gone home for the holidays. We like to fend for ourselves over Christmas. And we have a part-time gardener who comes twice a week.'

'Did you always have such a small staff?' asked Bell.

Abigail shook her head. 'When we were children, my parents had a whole team of gardeners and maids and chauffeurs, but Benjamin prefers – preferred – to live a little more simply.'

'I think I would like to speak to the maid first,' said Bell. 'And with all due respect, you might then leave us. I find that staff are reluctant to tell the whole truth in front of their employer.'

While he waited, Bell walked around the outer perimeter of the room, deep in thought about furnishings and window latches. Abigail soon returned with Dorcas in tow. She was a middle-aged woman who looked older than her years due to the greyness of her hair and the length of her heavy skirt. She looked, Bell thought approvingly, like a good old-fashioned servant.

'Please take a seat, Dorcas. I am Auguste Bell, consulting detective. You may call me Bell or whatever you are happy with.'

Dorcas reluctantly took a seat and Abigail left the room.

'How long have you worked for the family?' Bell asked. He was trying to put her at ease.

'Oh it's, let's see – twenty-eight years,' said Dorcas.

'It speaks so much to your loyal nature that you have remained in service to one family for so long,' Bell said.

Dorcas relaxed a little. 'Very kind of you to say so, sir. I think that loyalty goes both ways. After the death of the mistress and then of the master, Abigail and Benjamin have shown great loyalty in keeping me on.'

'You must have known both of them as children,' said Bell.

'Oh yes, I've known them nearly their whole lives. They are fine people. Their parents would be very proud.'

'Do you enjoy your job?'

'Very much so. I was born into service. And my parents before me. So few young people today are interested in a life in service. I think it seems too much like hard work for them.' She sniffed contemptuously.

Bell took a seat opposite her.

'Now, I know it will be very upsetting for you, but I must ask you to answer any questions I have for you in a full and frank manner. There will be no recriminations. Your knowledge, however insignificant the information might seem, can only be helpful to me. Now, can you tell me what happened yesterday?'

'It was a usual day. I went about my duties, readying the bedrooms for the guests and airing out the downstairs rooms. The guests started arriving from about two thirty. I was only here until about supper time. Abigail is very good about allowing me my free time. I went home and then had a nice dinner and a glass of wine at my sister's house. She made a shepherd's pie, which was a little under-seasoned for my liking, but I'm happy for the company all the same. And anyway, I think that Abigail and Benjamin wanted to be alone for the evening with their friends.'

'Did anything happen during the day? Anything to do with Benjamin?' he asked.

'No,' said Dorcas. 'Nothing I can think of.'

Bell felt instinctively that she was holding something back from him.

'Nothing at all? I beg of you, dear Dorcas. If you know something it is best to tell me immediately,' Bell said.

'There was a quarrel,' Dorcas said stiffly.

'A quarrel? Tell me about it,' said Bell.

Dorcas shifted in her chair.

'I'm not quite sure what it was,' she said. 'Might not have been a quarrel. I'm not sure what I heard, in fact.'

Bell was stern then. 'I appreciate your loyalty, but it is time for the truth. I think you know exactly what you heard.'

Dorcas was a little taken aback.

'Well, sir, I suppose things have changed. You are right. There was a quarrel between Benjamin and Stephen.'

'And what was the row about?' asked Bell.

'I want to be clear that I am not in the habit of listening outside closed doors.'

'Of course not.'

'I couldn't hear what was being said – it was muffled – but I could hear Stephen's voice and it was very loud. I like Stephen. Always polite. Used to come around to the house as a boy. But I think he can be a little hot-headed at times. He can lose the run of himself. It can be difficult being friends with Benjamin – things come so easily to him. I was tidying up in the drawing room, which happens to be next to Benjamin's office and that's how I heard the row. I am not a gossip.'

'Of course not, Dorcas. And what time did this quarrel occur?'

Dorcas thought for a moment.

'It happened just after I had helped clear away the lunch things, so it must have been a little after three o'clock.'

'And you are sure that the voices you heard were Benjamin and Stephen?'

'Oh, of course sir. I've known them since they were boys.'

'Thank you, Dorcas, that is all I have to ask you.' He rose from his seat, and prompted her to do the same.

Dorcas started to get up slowly from her seat. 'I hope I haven't said anything out of turn. I like Stephen – he's a good boy. He would never have done anything . . . bad, like that.'

'I understand,' said Bell.

She turned to leave, but then stopped. 'Will you be interviewing all the house guests, sir?' she asked.

'Yes, as part of my investigations.'

'Well, when you talk to Declan tell him that if he returns it by the end of today, I won't say anything to Abigail. Please tell him that, will you.'

Bell was mystified.

'Yes, tell him to return Mr Hudson's screwdriver without any fuss,' Dorcas said.

'Screwdriver?'

'Yes, Mr Hudson's. The gardener. Though he only comes Tuesdays and Fridays now. They used to have three full-time gardeners, but I suppose times change. Just before dinner, I saw it with my very own eyes – Declan rifling about in Mr Hudson's shed and when I checked, the small screwdriver was missing from its usual home. I don't know what he could be doing with it. Up to no good, I'm sure. I like Stephen, he's a good boy, but that Declan was always trouble, even as a child. It wasn't the murder weapon, by any chance?'

'No, madame. Not at all. But I will ask Declan about this. Oh, and just before you go – have any of the female guests complained to you that they are missing an earring?'

Dorcas looked confused.

'No. No one has said anything to me.'

'Well then, that will be all,' Bell said. 'Perhaps you would be so kind as to send in Mr O'Brien.'

*

Mr O'Brien, the butler, was a discreet, curt individual who did not appreciate being interviewed in this manner. Bell felt that he would not be as easy to manipulate as the maid and so he didn't even try.

Bell recounted what had been told to him by Dorcas and

his understanding of the sequence of events from the night before.

'Tell me, when did you retire to your own quarters?'

'At about eleven p.m. Abigail told me that they wouldn't need me again until the morning. I read for an hour or so – I could hear the celebrations at midnight and then went to sleep.'

'Did you wake at all during the night?' Bell asked.

'No,' O'Brien replied. 'I am a very sound sleeper.'

That was Bell's impression exactly.

'And this quarrel – did Dorcas mention anything to you about it?'

Mr O'Brien sighed.

'Dorcas has a great imagination. She exaggerates things. I would be wary of anything she told you. Whatever quarrel she overheard probably wasn't as bad as she imagined it to be.'

'She seemed pretty confident of what she had heard,' said Bell.

'I think she might have wanted to impress you. Dorcas is a great reader of detective fiction. In fact, I believe she's even read some of your books.'

'Ah! Were you aware of any animosity between the house guests?'

Mr O'Brien considered the question.

'Benjamin has known Stephen, Cormac and Declan a long time and I am sure there were rows over the years, but that is natural.'

'And of course, Margaret – their engagement was called off . . .'

'I am an old-fashioned type of person, I know. A trad-itionalist. My ideas would be mocked now. But I believe some things to be right and fair. Whatever went on between Benjamin and Margaret is none of my business. The engage-ment was called off and perhaps he was right to do it. But to carry on with his secretary and invite Margaret to witness it? It is just too much. It is very unlike the Benjamin I know—'

Mr O'Brien broke off, and set his face as though to give the impression of someone who had slipped up, but Bell was sure that Mr O'Brien had never made a single mistake in his professional life. What he was saying right now was very much on purpose.

'By secretary, you mean Barbara?'

'Yes. I'm sure she is a fine young woman, but she's got her-self into a bit of a mess now.'

'They were having an affair?'

'Whatever you would call it. Why else would he invite her to the party?'

'Perhaps they are friends. Or maybe she was alone over the holidays?'

Mr O'Brien looked at Bell as though he was a complete imbecile.

'Yes, maybe that's it,' he said witheringly.

'Just one more question before I let you go – is there a spare key to the master bedroom or indeed a master key to unlock the door?' Bell asked.

Mr O'Brien confirmed that there wasn't, and Bell released him back to his work duties.

*

79

Bell once again took to walking the perimeter of the room. He had lots to consider. Abigail appeared in the doorway.

'Before I begin my interrogation of the guests,' Bell said, 'would you permit me to look in Benjamin's office?'

'Of course,' she replied, and led the way across the hallway. Bell stepped inside the small room, his eyes moving quickly over the objects therein. It was very neat and tidy; everything had its place.

'Benjamin worked in the city mainly,' said Abigail.

'But he used this office over the holidays?'

'Yes, that's right. He and Barbara.'

'I see.'

Bell tried the drawers in the desk: the bottom two were practically empty but the top one was locked.

'Do you have the key to this drawer?' he asked Abigail.

'Unfortunately, no. I never come in here. It's not my domain. Maybe it's somewhere on the desk?'

But the tidiness of the desk meant that there was nothing for the key to be hidden under. Bell looked around him. Behind the door was a coat hook, and a dark jacket hanging from it. Bell put his hand into the left pocket but found it empty and then the right one and – victory. He held aloft a small silver key. It fit perfectly into the lock of the drawer. Inside were some personal papers: a passport, birth certificate, their parents' marriage certificate and a small date book. He read back a few weeks, but nothing jumped out at him. There were two entries for the following day: 'ring FWC' and then below that an indecipherable scribble with a star next to it.

'Have you found something?' Abigail asked.

'Perhaps,' Bell said. 'Do you by any chance know what this might mean?'

Abigail looked at the note.

'No idea,' she said eventually.

Sincere sympathies to Abigail and family. May Benjamin rest in peace.

I went to university with Ben and though we hadn't seen each other in a couple of years, I was shocked by the news of his sudden death. I remember Ben as bright and funny and always a little bit ahead of the rest of us. He read every book first, knew the name of any song on the radio. I wondered over the years where he had ended up, confident that he had a great future ahead of him. I regret not trying to contact him in years past. My sincere condolences to Benjamin's family.

I am so terribly sorry for the loss of your brother, Abigail.

I have spent all morning trying to write something eloquent but every time I think of any happy memories involving Ben I just start crying. This has come as such a shock to me. I can't understand it. My thoughts are with his family.

Ní bheidh a leithéad arís ann.

So sorry for your tragic loss. So hard to comprehend. Rest in peace Benjamin.

Condolences to the family of Benjamin he will be a beautiful angel in heaven looking down on you always may his beautiful soul rest in peace.

I have known Benjamin and his family for most of his life. He was a lovely boy and a kind beautiful man. Wishing Benjamin a peaceful resting place now. He was clearly very loved by all.

Chapter Seven

THE ARRIVAL OF THE INSPECTOR

The doorbell rang and they looked to each other.

'Are we expecting someone?' Abigail asked.

Bell checked his watch.

'Ah! That will be Detective Inspector Ferret. It's about time he showed up. Could someone go and answer the door?'

But the butler was already there dealing with the expected guest. He led the detective inspector into the office and closed the door behind him.

'Ah, Inspector. My good friend. It has been too long,' exclaimed Bell, his arms outstretched.

'Hello, Bell,' said Ferret with his trademark stoicism. 'I suppose I'm not surprised you're here. Big old country pile seems like your type of thing.'

'In fact,' Bell said, 'it's been a couple of books since I've done a classic murder mystery. I've been abroad in sunnier climes a lot lately. Last time, I was on a submarine. A bit of an experiment that didn't quite work out. In fact, I think you are the one who is a bit out of your jurisdiction, Inspector. Are you investigating this case as well?'

'In a sense. I've been told by the local plod that this matter has been declared a suicide but once I heard you were involved, I assumed there had to be something more to it,' said the inspector.

'Yes, indeed. I am investigating a murder. This is Abigail, the deceased's sister.'

'Very sorry for your loss, ma'am,' said Ferret, removing his hat. 'The reason I'm really in the area is to check on a house just five miles from here. You probably haven't heard the news – what with everything – but there was a burglary there last night. They stole some jewellery and got into the safe. The man of the house woke up during the thing and he's got a nasty cut to the head.'

'Oh dear, will he be okay?' asked Abigail.

'The doctor's looking after him now. He and his wife are both in shock, as you might imagine, but they'll be all right. It's the third such burglary in this area in the past few months.'

'And you think it might be linked to our own tragic death?' Bell suggested.

'It's one theory I'm working on,' said the inspector. He turned to Abigail. 'Have you noticed anything missing? Any jewellery, cash etcetera?'

'No,' said Abigail. 'Nothing like that.'

'Do you happen to have a safe in the house?' the inspector asked.

'Yes, in fact it's in this room. Over there, hidden in the wall just behind you.'

The inspector stepped aside so Abigail could remove a painting of a river scene from the wall, revealing the safe door. He watched as she turned the dial and then opened it to inspect its contents.

'Nothing has been disturbed,' she confirmed before closing the safe again.

'What do you keep in there?' asked Bell.

'Mainly documents,' Abigail said. 'And some jewellery and watches that belonged to my parents. It's not very exciting.'

'I think I would like to continue with my interviews, Abigail. Could you please get Stephen and bring him to the library? I will show the inspector out.'

Abigail turned to go but stopped.

'Just one more thing,' she said. 'I could have sworn that in the night, I heard a noise. I wasn't sure if it was on the roof – sometimes the birds can be very loud – or just outside the house. I thought it was a dream but now I'm not so sure.'

'What kind of noise was it?' asked the inspector.

'It was like a thump, I suppose. Just a single thump. It was quiet after that.'

'Are you sure, mademoiselle,' asked Bell kindly, 'that you are not just hoping that you heard a noise? That would be very convenient for everyone. Do you wish that it was an outsider even after all I have told you?'

'Oh, you are probably right about that, yes, yes,' said Abigail. 'I just thought I should mention it. I don't know what information is pertinent and what isn't.'

'No, you were right to tell us. And if you think of anything else, please do not hesitate to inform me.'

At the front door, Bell asked Ferret: 'Do you really believe this was the work of a burglar?'

'It's just a theory we're working on, Bell. We're trying to figure this out, same as you.'

'We should keep each other informed,' said Bell. 'By the

way, what is your professional opinion of the local detective inspector? The gentleman was very resolute in declaring it a suicide.'

'I think he's a man who likes an easy life. Trust your instincts on this one,' said Ferret, before Bell bid him farewell.

Our sincere condolences to Abigail on the tragic and sudden passing of your dear brother. Thinking of you and all your extended family at this very difficult time. May he Rest In Peace.

Benjamin was a great friend, caring, loving, empathetic, a great listener. It is difficult to imagine that he is no longer with us. I last spoke to him a couple of weeks ago when he seemed in good spirits. I hope that he has found some peace at last.

Abigail, thinking of you in this difficult time. I have lit a candle for Benjamin. My heart is broken for you.

You don't know me but I saw the news of your brother's death and needed to say something. It has brought back memories of my own tragedy. Four years ago now. Another poor young man. As you will soon find out things will never be the same again. I manage to get out of bed every morning and get on with life. But it's not really living. It's just counting down the days until I can see him again.

My deepest sympathies. Sending you all strength at this difficult time. Suaimhneas síoraí dá anam.

On behalf of all the team, I would like to extend our condolences to Benjamin's family on his death. Benjamin was a capable and generous co-worker and a good friend to many of us. He will be missed.

Sincere condolences on the loss of Benjamin. May he rest in peace.

Thinking and praying for his family at this most difficult time.

Chapter Eight

THE EVIDENCE OF THE SCHOOL FRIEND

'Who are we interviewing next?' asked Sacker, emerging from an armchair in the corner of the library as if he had always been there.

'Ah, there you are Sacker!' said Bell. 'I've been waiting for you.'

'My arrival was delayed, so I was just catching up,' he replied, closing a small, battered paperback before slipping it into his inside jacket pocket. 'So, who's it going to be? The jilted ex-lover or the mistress?'

'I think we will start with Stephen,' said Bell.

'Oh no, Bell. That's far too boring. We need to sex this story up a little.'

Bell shook his head impatiently.

'But Stephen is the one who found that the door was locked, and of course there was the row overheard by the maid – it makes sense to interview him first,' said Bell.

'I suppose,' said Sacker, though he didn't sound convinced.

Stephen soon arrived with Abigail in tow. Bell was about to ask her to leave but he was struck by the closeness between them and thought it might be more informative if they both stayed. He invited them to sit down opposite him, and they did – each clasping their own hands, and leaning their bodies forward. Stephen had an easy-going handsomeness about him. Bell could see why Dorcas thought him charming.

'Thank you for coming to see me,' Bell said. 'I know this must be a stressful time for you. I will try not to keep you too long.'

Stephen nodded softly and glanced towards Sacker.

'And this is Sacker, of course. My sidekick – my associate – my Watson, you understand? You probably didn't see him earlier, but he serves an important literary function.* He'll come up with a series of ideas for which I will invariably mock him before one of his inane theories will spark something in me. He even gets in a bit of narration when needs be.'

'Of course,' said Stephen. 'How do you do?' He shook hands with Sacker. 'We are happy to have your assistance in this matter.'

'The first thing I will ask,' Bell continued, 'is whether you agree with the police's assessment of this case. Do you believe your friend killed himself?'

'No,' Stephen said, though his eyes flickered slightly. 'No, I don't – I mean, I can't imagine—'

'You never saw anything in Benjamin's demeanour to suggest that something might be amiss?'

'No.'

'Stephen was Benjamin's closest friend,' said Abigail. 'He would have known if something was wrong.'

---

* 'Let us know from chapter to chapter what the detective is thinking. For this he must watsonize or solilioquize . . .' A. A. Milne's introduction to *The Red House Mystery*.

'I will ask you – during the evening's festivities, did anything unusual happen? Did Benjamin mention anything? Did you discuss something important?'

Stephen shook his head.

'Nothing that stood out,' he said, but then there was that flicker again.

'Of course, you were the one who checked on Benjamin and found that his door was locked. Isn't that right? Tell me in your own words what happened this morning from the time you woke up.'

Stephen breathed out long and slow.

'I awoke, I don't know what time it was unfortunately. The night before – well it had been a party and I had been drinking so when I first opened my eyes initially, I didn't feel in the best of health. I laid in bed for a few minutes and then I went to have a shower, brush my teeth, that sort of thing. Tried to make myself feel human again. I got dressed and came downstairs for breakfast – we realized at some point that Benjamin wasn't there and so . . .'

He stopped then, and looked to Abigail to continue for him.

'Stephen went upstairs to wake him,' Abigail began. 'The door was locked and . . .'

They both went quiet, and Abigail took Stephen's hand in hers. They looked very much like a couple, Bell thought.

'You have known each other a long time,' Bell said quietly. 'It must be a great comfort to the both of you.' He wanted to try something. He wanted to push. 'What did you row about earlier in the evening?' Bell said.

Stephen stared at him.

'You were overheard arguing in his office before dinner,' Bell explained.

'Overheard by whom?' asked Stephen.

'Ah, so you did have a row,' said Bell.

'A row?' asked Abigail, mystified.

'It was nothing,' said Stephen dismissively.

'Please tell me what happened,' Bell said.

'Well,' Stephen began, and he shared a tiny glance with Abigail. 'Benjamin and I had a little argument earlier in the evening – it was a silly thing really. My fault and not something to quarrel over. But it was— It has nothing to do with what happened. That's why I didn't bother mentioning it. It had nothing to do with his – with his death.'

'I think that's for me to decide,' said Bell gravely.

'It wasn't that serious, honestly; it was just a tiff. I nearly didn't come to the party. I was on the outs with him, but my girlfriend convinced me to come. Said it would be good to catch up.'

Bell noticed Abigail stiffening at the mention of the word 'girlfriend'.

'The maid said that it was a very loud argument,' said Bell.

'The maid—' said Stephen. 'Maybe it was. Benjamin and I are both very emotional people. A little volatile perhaps. We can lose our heads sometimes.'

'Did you argue a lot with Benjamin?' asked Bell.

'We've known each other such a long time,' Stephen said. 'We can't be best friends every day or every week. Have you never argued with a friend? I just felt he wasn't pulling his weight. He's been ducking my phone calls. It was all

becoming a little one-sided. I tried with him but he always—
It seems so silly now. It really doesn't matter.'

'Stephen would never hurt Benjamin,' Abigail said.
'You can take it from me. Whatever this row was, it was
inconsequential.'

'In fact,' Stephen continued, his eyes suddenly alight, 'as I
was going to bed – I don't know if it was the alcohol making
me sentimental – but I thought I might apologize to him if
he was still awake. So, I tried his door, and it was locked. I
suppose you won't believe me. But it's the truth. I loved him.
He was my best friend.'

Stephen started to sob then, and Abigail held him to her.

*

'What do you make of that?' asked Sacker once they had both
gone.

'It's difficult to say,' said Bell. 'Abigail certainly seems to
believe him.'

Sacker sat down next to him and put his feet up on the
table.

'I don't like good-looking people,' complained Sacker. 'It is
so difficult to tell when they're lying. Especially the women.'

'If only they'd made you a doctor, dear Sacker,' said Bell,
casting him a withering glance. 'It would have at least given
you some respectability.'

To: Abigail
From: Airbnb
Re: Rate your stay
Date: 5 January 2023

You just checked out of Yew Tree House. Take a few minutes to rate your stay and let your host know how they did.

You'll have the chance to leave private feedback just for your host, plus write a public review that'll appear on their listing's page and help future guests know what to expect.

We won't share anything you say with Brian until they write a review too.

Chapter Nine

A VISIT FROM THE AUNT

A large car had pulled into the driveway and screeched to a halt in front of the house. Soon after, there was an explosion of noise from the hallway: a violent knocking at the front door, then a woman's booming voice and finally Abigail.

Bell and Sacker went into the hallway to investigate. There they were met with the sight of a small grey-haired woman hugging and pawing at poor Abigail. She stopped once she saw Bell.

'Mr O'Brien,' the woman said, 'you've put on a lot of weight.'

'Oh no, aunt. That isn't the butler. This is Auguste Bell, the famous detective,' said Abigail, a little embarrassed.

'No need to worry, madame,' said Bell. 'I am pleased to make your acquaintance, though of course I wish it wasn't in such terrible circumstances.'

'A detective?' the aunt cried out. 'Oh Abigail, why have you hired a detective? Such a low thing to do. You know better than that.'

'Bell is very well thought of,' said Abigail.

'Well, I've never heard of him,' said the aunt. 'And I know everyone.'

'Bell is rather a famous man,' explained Sacker. 'He has solved some of the world's most famous murders.'

'Murder!' declared the aunt. 'But I thought this was a dreadful suicide. Though I don't know which is worse.'

Abigail linked arms with her aunt and started to draw her away.

'I'll take you upstairs to get settled,' Abigail said. 'Will I get someone to bring in your bags?'

'Oh no, dear. I'm not staying,' said the aunt. 'Oh no, the whole thing is far too upsetting for me.'

'But surely, you'll stay. I mean, where else would you go?' asked Abigail.

'I am staying nearby with my good friends the Mallowans. You know them – I think you went horse-riding with their daughter. I just called in to see you. You should come with me, Abigail. It is sinister to stay in a house where somebody died. Doesn't it unnerve you?'

'I have to stay until the investigation is over,' Abigail said. 'I can't leave now.'

'Oh dear,' said the aunt. 'You were always so rational, even as a child. Always needing an explanation for everything. But you can't stay in here for ever. You will have to rejoin the real world at some stage.' She checked her watch. 'I can see that I won't be able to dissuade you for now. I will call again in a couple of days and hopefully this whole thing will be over by then. And I will leave this candle with you; it will help to cleanse the house of evil spirits.' Abigail accepted the large candle as her aunt eyed Bell. 'Harrumph,' she said. 'Well, you know where to find me, dear.'

*

'She is quite the character,' said Bell once the aunt had zoomed down the drive again.

'I feel I should apologize for her,' Abigail said. 'She can be quite overwhelming. Like a hurricane. But she means well.'

'Oh, there is no need to apologize for family,' Bell said.

'She is the only relative we have and so while she can be a handful it is important for me to keep contact with her,' said Abigail. 'Though having said that, it's probably best that she's not staying. I would only have had to look after her.'

'Do the Mallowans live far from here?' asked Bell.

'Just about a fifteen-minute car journey up the road. Our land abuts theirs, though I don't really know them that well. People around here don't socialize with each other,' said Abigail. 'Maybe I did horse-ride with their daughter, but I can't remember now.'

*

A t the removal, she sits next to her aunt and shakes hands with wave upon wave of people. Some she recognizes; many others she doesn't. A lot are her parents' friends: people whose faces she knows but whose names have disappeared with the years. Then neighbours. Co-workers. A woman who babysat them as children. Old family friends. A parade of beautiful young women: old girlfriends and dates. One in particular whose name she can't remember and who dated her brother for all of six months wails at her and hugs her and has to be led away by two friends. She sees Margaret raise her eyes to the heavens as the woman passes. Benjamin would have found this so funny and that thought makes her feel very sad. Barbara is there, tentative, and polite. Abigail shakes hands with her as if they are nothing more than strangers – which they are, of course. They just happen to share this single thing – this odd overlapping of their lives. And then Stephen and his girlfriend. He is pale and his eyes are red. His girlfriend has one arm clutched around him, practically holding him up. She guides him through the funeral home. As they pass by Abigail, Stephen has his head turned so that he can see the coffin. He grips his girlfriend tighter and lets out a tiny cry. Abigail wants to reach out to him. The next person is already there, and she is shaking hands and accepting condolences again. And soon Declan is there looking flustered. Declan's tiny mother grasps her and kisses her and says, 'thank god your parents aren't here' and Abigail just has to take it. Cormac and a whole bunch of other people who had gone to college with Benjamin walk by, each of them treating her like an old maid. Then old friends of hers – people she had gone to school with, others she had played camogie with, former co-workers, someone from university she hadn't spoken to in years. And she is touched that they have all turned up. That they had even seen the notice. Her life is so full of people really and for a moment she feels both exhausted and replenished by them. Eventually, the queue of people wanes, and Abigail is afforded some time to breathe. Afterwards, she drives her aunt back home and accepts her offer to come and have a slice of cake and some tea. Abigail isn't hungry but she hasn't eaten all day. Her aunt is saying, 'isn't it nice that so-and-so made it I haven't seen them in years' and 'god blah-de-blah has got so old suddenly.' They talk about the next day: the funeral. Her aunt wants to know if she has her eulogy ready. 'I don't want to call it a eulogy,' Abigail says. 'That makes it sound very grand.' Her aunt is carefully slicing a Tunisian orange cake that a neighbour dropped in. 'That's okay, dear,' she says, handing her a slice on a small plate. 'It can be whatever you want it to be. You don't have to say everything you are feeling in one go.'

Later, at home, she suddenly remembers the photograph. She opens the WhatsApp group, which hasn't been in use in over a week, and selects the photo Stephen had sent her.

Everyone looks so happy. She zooms in on Benjamin. The lower part of his face is obscured by Barbara's hair so she can't tell if he is smiling. His arms are by his sides. His eyes are neutral. Whatever it is she is looking for, she won't find it here.

Chapter Ten

THE EVIDENCE OF THE FORMER FIANCÉE

Being surrounded by all these young people made Bell contemplate his own youth, which he could now see he had completely wasted. He should have been more adventurous, he should have taken more chances, fallen in love, gained enemies. Watching this group – even now in its darkest days – he envied them the time they had. What did he have to show for it all? The choices he made in his early life had not made him a better detective. They had not made him happy.

'Did you hear me?' asked Sacker.

'I'm sorry, dear Sacker. I was thinking about my younger days,' said Bell.

'It's unlike you to be stuck in the past,' said Sacker.

'Being around all these young people has made me nostalgic,' said Bell.

'Steady on. Are you feeling unwell?'

'Oh, I'm feeling fine. I just find my mind wandering . . .'

'Well, if I could help to quell the wandering for a moment, I was just going to ask what the next steps were.'

'Oh, yes, of course,' said Bell.

Abigail appeared at the library door.

'Remind me,' Bell asked her, 'who travelled from the city with your brother yesterday?'

'Benjamin drove down with Declan and Margaret,' Abigail replied.

'Ah, yes. Margaret, the former fiancée. You might please send her in next.'

Abigail did as she was told, and Margaret duly presented herself for interview. Her manner was neat and tidy and very much in control of herself.

Bell asked her to recount the events of the previous forty-eight hours and she did so in a series of precise factual statements. She was not one to make assumptions or to pass comment. She kept her counsel.

'I met Benjamin when I was twenty – we were both twenty. We were friends for a while and then a relationship developed between us. We were together for three, three and a half years. And we were engaged for about a year of that. We hadn't started planning the wedding, though. That was probably a bad sign. We broke up but remained on good terms. Which I am glad of. Especially now. He was an important person in my life.'

'At the time of his death, were you still only . . . friends?' Bell asked.

'Yes, yes, just that.'

She didn't fit the profile of the jilted lover, Bell thought to himself.

'And can you talk me through your own movements between, say, midnight and nine a.m. this morning?'

'At midnight, I was with everyone outside, celebrating the New Year. After the fireworks, I was indoors with the others until, I think, two o'clock or thereabouts, when I went upstairs to bed. I fell asleep at some point, and I awoke sometime after nine. I can't be too sure. I didn't check my watch.'

'Did you look in on Benjamin before you went to sleep? Or indeed, before you came downstairs?'

'No,' said Margaret simply.

'Did you speak to Benjamin during the night?'

She sniffed. 'We spoke a little. It wasn't really a talking kind of evening. It was a celebratory type of evening.'

'After your engagement was called off, did you often socialize with Benjamin? I mean, was it unusual for you to be invited to his birthday party?'

'Not unusual. We remained on good terms. And I'm friends with Abigail so she always invites me to New Year's bashes and summer dos'.

'What was the reason for the break-up?'

Margaret bristled.

'Is that pertinent?'

'It might be. It is important to gather all the information and then sift through it to find what makes sense.'

'Well, it wasn't anything very exciting. We just . . . drifted apart. We'd been together since we were young. And people get older and they change. Our lives were going in different directions.'

Bell felt that there was a rehearsed air to her response. How many times had she performed this monologue?

'So, the break-up was amicable?'

'Yes,' said Margaret with finality. He would get nothing more out of her on this matter.

'I understand that you travelled with Benjamin and Declan,'

said Bell. 'Did anything come up in conversation during the drive down?'

'Not really. I mean, there was the usual stuff from Declan about money—'

'Money?' said Sacker. Suddenly he was interested.

'Yes, Declan is an awful gambler, and I mean awful in the sense that he always loses. Benjamin is constantly having to bail him out, but he put his foot down this time and refused to give him another loan. Good thing, too. I told him to do it years ago,' said Margaret.

'Sounds like a motive,' Sacker said.

'Oh, dear god!' Margaret exclaimed. 'That's not what I was getting at, at all.'

'You don't believe that Declan could be capable of such a thing?'

'Of course not. Declan is a dolt. Harmless. It is absolutely ridiculous.'

'Is there anything else that happened over the past twenty-four hours, anything you feel you should bring to my attention?'

Margaret's eyes moved around the room.

'I can't really think. I mean, this whole thing has been such a nightmare. Well, I suppose . . .' She paused. 'I suppose the only thing that sticks out as unusual was that phone call Barbara made late afternoon yesterday in Benjamin's office.'

'And what was it about this phone call that made it stick in your memory?'

'I couldn't hear what she was saying. She was speaking very low. But there was something about her tone that threw me. It didn't really sound like her. Not that I know her well. None of us do. But she sounded quite strict. And maybe a little angry. And afterwards I thought she seemed a little upset.'

'And what time, mademoiselle, did you overhear this conversation?'

'Oh, it was just as I was going up to change for dinner, so between six p.m. and six thirty, perhaps. You understand I wasn't trying to overhear anything. It was just by accident.'

'Of course.' Bell smiled widely at her. 'And do you know if Barbara made the phone call or did she answer a call?'

'Oh, she made the call. Definitely. I would have heard it ring otherwise.'

'Perhaps this was a professional call on behalf of Benjamin? They had been working earlier in the day.'

Margaret's eyes narrowed. 'Perhaps,' she said carefully.

'Were you surprised to see that Benjamin had invited Barbara along to the party?'

Margaret's jaw tensed.

'Not surprised at all.'

'You were anticipating it?'

'No. I wouldn't say that, but Benjamin is a . . . very generous employer.' She sniffed again. 'I think I have told you absolutely anything and everything I could think of, so if you would excuse me, I'm sure Abigail needs me.'

'Yes, of course. That will be all for now.'

As Bell contemplated all that had been told to him, his hand drifted to his pocket. He removed the single gold earring.

'Just one more thing – do you recognize this?' said Bell.

Margaret squinted at it.

'No,' she said finally. 'Is it important?'

Bell didn't answer.

'Did you notice anyone wearing these earrings last night? Please look at it carefully.'

'I honestly don't know,' said Margaret eventually.

'Ah, well, I will let you go,' said Bell.

*

'At last, things have got going,' said Sacker. 'Money! Dalliances! Intrigue!'

'I thought this might excite you,' said Bell.

'I had been a little bit worried that this was going to be dull, like *The Clue of the Scarlet Petal*,' said Sacker. 'I had to absent myself from the second half of that one.'

'Ah yes, you were knocked unconscious, weren't you?' said Bell.

'Yes, came to just after the reveal. It helped solve the crime though, didn't it?' said Sacker. 'That thing about Barbara and the phone call was interesting, though of course we have no witnesses to it. She could have made it all up.'

'Indeed,' Bell replied. 'But I think that even the lies that are told to me are interesting, don't you agree?'

*

The funeral is filled with music. Stephen has picked out some of Benjamin's favourite songs and they sit there in sad silence listening to them. Then there is a series of readings, of poems, of remembrances. She had invited Declan to speak but he didn't want to, and Abigail didn't push the matter. Stephen reads a poem. A series of work friends say a few words. Cormac reads an extract from Benjamin's favourite book and Margaret shares some photographs and memories – Benjamin sunburned in a kayak; Benjamin and Margaret in black tie in a photograph taken by his father; Benjamin in a pub smiling dreamily at the camera. And then Abigail gets up to speak. Right now, looking down at the words on the page, she hates what she has written. It's too sentimental, too impersonal, none of this sounds like her or like Benjamin. Everything sounds like a cliché. Like a lie. She finds that she doesn't know how to describe who her brother is in the wake of his death. It is as though all the happy memories have fallen out of her head. After she has finished, she sits back down next to her aunt. Margaret, sitting in the row behind, leans forward and squeezes her shoulder. The funeral director comes over to her after a little time and asks if they are ready to go. Ready to go to the graveyard is what he means. Ready to deposit her brother's body into the earth. She says she is ready even though she isn't. How could she ever be ready? Cormac, Stephen, Declan and three others get up and deal with the coffin. It goes out and she follows it, her arm interlocked with her aunt's and the rest following behind them. The coffin slides into the hearse, and it feels like an ending. Her chest tightens a little. Her childhood is in that box. The memories of her parents, of every Christmas morning, every trip to the beach. A short car journey to the graveyard – she won't remember it after, won't remember if she drove or if someone else did, what car did they take? – and then they are walking towards her parents' grave. It is windy in the way that it is always windy in graveyards, always cold even on the warmest of days. Everyone is windswept and sombre. But she likes the bracing weather. It feels like life. It is only as they are lowering the coffin into the grave that she realizes. Three coffins. It is full now. It is as if something has hit her square in the chest. She tries to swallow and feels herself choke. She tries to pull air into her lungs but can't. Her aunt, who is holding her, encloses her further, which makes things worse. She can't breathe. It is as though her lungs have deflated. She tries to draw air in through her nose but can't. Her aunt realizes that something is wrong and lets her go. 'What's happening?' she asks and finally, like a crack of sunlight through a curtain, a small amount of air gets through. She inhales again, one hand on her aunt's shoulder, and more space opens up in her chest. It takes her five more deep breaths before she is feeling somewhat normal. Her hand shakes. 'I couldn't breathe,' she croaks. The funeral director has arrived with a bottle of water, and she sips it nervously. People are looking; she is making a scene. 'You need to sit down somewhere. It's the stress,' says her aunt. 'No, no, I'm fine,' says Abigail. 'Are we . . . ready?' asks the funeral director. Her aunt nods on her behalf. Margaret is there now and all three stand clutching each other, holding each other up as the coffin is released and they, in silence, allow it to happen. It's done now, she thinks. 'What happened?' asks Margaret. 'I think she had a panic attack,' her aunt says. Margaret practically carries Abigail to a nearby bench and then stands over her, looming, unsure. Abigail feels she needs to say something now, even if it doesn't make sense. She just needs someone to know. 'I want to be cremated,' she says. 'And my ashes scattered over the grave. Don't bury me somewhere else.' Margaret just nods. 'I want to be cremated,' she repeats. Her voice is a croaky whisper. 'Don't bury me by myself.'

Chapter Eleven

THE EVIDENCE OF THE EMPLOYEE

'Ah, the mistress!' declared Sacker. 'Now things are really starting to get exciting.'

Bell exhaled loudly. Sacker had no respect for the method. He was all about the glamourous moments, wanting excitement, titillation and adventure. Bell liked things to slowly rise to the surface. But, he supposed, that's why Sacker was so useful; it was because they were both such different characters.

'Please go fetch Barbara and bring her here,' Bell said, and Sacker practically skipped out of the room. He returned with her quickly, closing the doors behind her with a flourish.

'Ah, Barbara. Thank you for coming to see me. Please take a seat here. I hope it is comfortable for you.'

Barbara took a seat and nodded at both men.

'It would seem to me,' Bell said very carefully, 'that you have a special insight into this matter we are currently investigating.'

Barbara looked a little frightened.

'I don't know— I don't think— How could I?'

'What I mean by this is – not to impugn you in any way – but to point out that you have a knowledge of the deceased that no one else has.'

Barbara just stared.

'Because you work together, and you are the only one who sees him day in, day out in that specific environment. Secretaries know so much about their employers.'

'Well, I suppose that might be true,' said Barbara, relaxing noticeably, 'but I don't think I have any information that might help you with your investigations.'

'You don't need to be bonded at the hip to have gained some insight. Did Benjamin have any worries? Any concerns? Any financial difficulties?'

'He was not a man who worried particularly. He was very in control, very stable. I don't know anything about finances. That wasn't my department. But the business seemed sound, always. I've been happy working there.'

'Did it seem unusual to you that your employer would invite you to his private residence for New Year's?'

She paused before she spoke. Bell noticed that everyone he had interviewed so far was being careful with their words.

'Yes, it did a little, but then Benjamin has always been good to me. I am unmarried and I have no children. My father died when I was young, and my mother was moved to a nursing home recently after her health deteriorated and I could no longer take care of her. Benjamin knew all this. This was a little holiday for me. But also, of course, we had work to do.'

'Yes, you were in his office yesterday for a time.'

'He had some letters he needed typed up.'

'What letters?'

'Just some business letters. Nothing scandalous.'

'You can see how this looks, mademoiselle.'

'What do you mean?' she asked, and Bell thought he saw genuine confusion on her face.

'A man bringing his secretary to a shindig in his country house. It looks like he was having an affair,' he said gently.

'Oh,' said Barbara, looking truly aghast. 'Oh, it didn't even occur to me. Is that what everyone thinks?'

'I can't tell you what everyone thinks. But I suspect that it is a topic of conversation amongst the rest of the guests.'

'Well, I— You will need to make it plain to them that I— Oh dear . . .'

'I take it, then, that there was nothing romantic going on between you and Benjamin,' said Bell.

'Oh no, of course not,' Barbara said.

'Because I will say, if something was going on, I will find out about it. There is no point in lying. Especially not now.'

But Barbara maintained her position vehemently.

'This whole thing must be very odd for you,' said Bell.

'Well, it is odd for all of us. We are not famous consulting detectives. We are not used to things like murder.'

'What I mean is that you are a stranger to the others. They are a comfort to each other, whereas you only have yourself. You must feel a little bit alone in this house,' Bell said.

'Oh, it's not that bad. It seems silly to complain about something like that right now.'

'But you are not complaining. I am merely pointing out how you must feel. Everyone has their person here but you. Don't worry, we won't keep you much longer. Is there anything else you can think of that might be of some assistance? Any pertinent information?' Bell asked.

'Well, I remember, at least I think I remember, that during the night someone tried to get into my room.'

'Tell me more, mademoiselle. This could be very important.'

'I was awoken— Well, to be honest I thought in the morning it was a dream – it can be difficult to tell in the middle of the night what is real and what is not. But I am fairly certain that sometime during the very early morning someone tried the doorknob to my bedroom. It was locked, of course. I always lock my door. That's all really. I'm not sure what use it is.'

'All information is useful,' said Bell.

*

'She was a bit of a disappointing mistress,' Sacker said. 'In fact, not a mistress at all. What a waste.'

'You believe her story?' asked Bell.

'You don't?' responded Sacker.

'I believe that she was not in a romantic relationship with Benjamin,' Bell said carefully.

'Well then, what do you think the old fellow was up to? Was he genuinely such a kind but foolish man or was he trying to cause a scandal?' Sacker asked.

'That, for once, is a very astute question, Sacker.'

*

Her aunt had insisted on paying for the meal in a local hotel after the funeral. She had told Abigail that you had to feed people when they travel to a funeral, it was the correct thing to do. After her mother had died, they didn't have any meal. They just drove home with their father and the house was so empty and cold and she went to bed at five o'clock but never really slept again. That was when she began to hate the house. She tried to spend as much time outside of it as possible. She joined every sports team and every school club. She volunteered at weekends and got a part-time job when she turned sixteen. She hung around shopping centres and slept over at friends' as often as she could. Something had changed about the place she called home, and she would never be able to return to it as a place of comfort again. When her father died, she and Benjamin had organized a meal, because that seemed like the grown-up thing to do. They had sold the house after that. It didn't suit either of them and their feelings towards it had become distant. It didn't feel like a family home. They split the proceeds between them and got their own places. She loved her house. It was her space. Whenever she was away travelling for a while and came back to it, she had that feeling she had always wanted – of home. Once, years ago, she had driven out to their old house, to their family home. She pulled in her car across the way and watched it: the new owners had put in more modern double-glazed windows and had done some work to the garden. The gate was painted green and there was a new front door. She felt no pang, no feeling of familiarity. And she was happy about that, happy that they had not made a mistake in selling it. You can never go back. That's the thing. You can never go back. It would be a mistake even to try. She never called to the house again. It wasn't hers anymore, it never had been, really. She turned the car around and drove back – home.

Chapter Twelve

THE EVIDENCE OF THE CHILDHOOD FRIEND

'I'm sure you've heard all sorts about me,' Declan said before he had even taken his seat. 'And all of it is true.' He laughed then, a big booming laugh that filled the room.

'I have heard one or two . . . let's say less than complimentary things,' confirmed Bell. 'But I am a methodical man and I never make any final judgement until I am sure. I make my own mind up about things. You will have plenty of time to show me that they are wrong.'

'That's the thing, though. They probably aren't wrong. Not really,' said Declan with a sigh. 'I've made a bit of a mess of my life. And I only have myself to blame for it.'

'Please tell me everything.'

Declan puffed out his cheeks and then let the air escape gently through his pursed lips.

'Well, I'm not as well off as Ab and Benj. I mean, don't get me wrong, my parents do well for themselves, but my childhood was nothing like this. There wasn't any family business to take over. And I lucked out by being friends with Benjamin and being brought along on holidays and getting used to a certain type of living. But I got too used to it. I burned through my trust fund very quickly and my parents refused to bail me out. They've cut me off, in fact. But Benj was always good to me. Always stuck by me. Got me a job and then I messed that up. Got me another job and I messed that up too.'

'And the gambling debts . . . ?'

'Oh, you've heard about that, have you? Well, yes, I enjoy a flutter. More than a flutter. And Benj has bailed me out so many times. I took him for granted.' Declan's voice started to crack a little. 'I suppose I was jealous of all that he had. Of how easy everything was for him. I felt that he owed me something for all his good luck.'

'But he cut you off?'

'That's right. He got sick of me, like everyone does in the end. He stuck with me longer than most, in fairness to him. But he refused to give me another loan. I was very angry and— Oh, I know exactly how it looks – that's why I'm being so up-front about my flaws. I would never— I mean, we have an argument about money and then he turns up dead, but I swear I would never— I'm a prat, but I'm not a killer.'

Bell nodded his head.

'You slept downstairs last night. Is this right?'

'Yes, I had too much to drink. I was feeling sorry for myself. And frankly I figured that I might never get invited to a party here again so I should probably have all my fun now. I fell asleep in the drawing room – I don't remember the time.'

'Did you wake up at any point?'

'Once. Not sure when but the house was quiet. Needed to piss.'

'So, you went upstairs?' Bell said.

'My mind is a little foggy on the exact details but after I used the facilities, I tried to find my room, but I got a bit lost – I'm not used to such a big house – so I came back downstairs and fell asleep on the sofa again. Next thing I know I could smell breakfast cooking and then after that noise from upstairs.'

'Do you recall anything out of the ordinary during your night-time walkabout?'

'No,' Declan said. 'Everyone was asleep as far as I could tell. It was very quiet. I was a bit out of it, to be honest. I have a lot of bruises on my legs. Must have bumped into a couple of things during the night. And I couldn't figure out which room was mine, like I said. I tried a couple of doors . . .' His voice trailed away then and his eyes became glassy, as though he was thinking about something else.

'Ah, of course. And can you think of who may have killed Benjamin?'

Declan's mind was elsewhere.

'Sorry, what?' he said.

'Do you have any suspicions as regards the murderer?'

'Oh,' said Declan, waking from his daydream. 'No. No, I don't.'

Bell watched him carefully. 'I have also been asked to pass on a message for you,' he said.

'A message for me?'

'Yes, from Dorcas.'

Declan's face was filled with genuine confusion.

'The maid,' explained Bell.

'Oh, yes, old Doris,' said Declan. 'Of course.'

'She has told me to tell you that if you replace the gardener's screwdriver by the end of the day, she won't say anything to Abigail.'

'*Replace the gardener's screwdriver*,' repeated Declan. 'Is that a euphemism?'

'You don't know what she is referring to?' asked Bell.

'Not an iota,' said Declan.

'Well, that will be all for now, Declan. If we need you again, we will call.'

*

'Pretty up-front sort of chap,' said Sacker, rising from his armchair in the corner of the library once Declan had left the room. 'Very honest about himself.'

'Indeed. And he admits freely to going upstairs, which would account for the noises that awoke Barbara in the night. Why would he admit to that if he were the killer?'

'Of course, it could be a double bluff to try and put us off the scent,' said Sacker. 'He could be trying to fool us.'

'I will reserve my judgement on Declan for now,' said Bell.

To: Abigail
From: Coroner's office
Re: personal details
Date: 18 January 2023

Thank you for your email. I would appreciate it if you would forward the following details by post/email (please record 'personal details' in the subject line of your email), for the completion of the ultimate Death Certificate:

Full birth name

Home address

Date and place of birth

Marital Status: Single/Married/Widowed/Divorced/Legally Separated

Occupation of deceased (if retired please state previous occupation)

Occupation of spouse (if applicable)

GP and Consultant's name, address, and telephone number

PPS number

Father's name

Mother's name (including maiden name if applicable)

Next of kin details: name, address, telephone number

Person to contact if different from next of kin

As you are aware, a complete death certificate will only be issued when this office is in receipt of the post-mortem report. Current timeline for the issue of post-mortem reports is as follows:

10–12 weeks if your family member was an inpatient in hospital at the time of their demise

4–5 months for all other circumstances; for example, where a loved one dies at his/her home or in another residence.

Chapter Thirteen

BELL AND SACKER GO TO AN INN

'Do you think it's safe to leave them alone for the night?' Sacker asked as they stood in the hallway waiting for the cab that would bring them to the inn.

'Of course. This is very much a single-dead-body story. We have nothing to fear.'

Soon, their cab arrived. They both bundled into the back seat and the driver set off down the long driveway, and then onto the meandering country road until they arrived at a pretty building, like a house from a chocolate box. They were met at the door by the inn's landlady, who insisted on helping with their bags and coats and then encouraged them to come and sit by the roaring fire. They were happy to oblige.

'Will I get you something hot to drink?' she asked them, and they said yes. She soon returned with mugs of hot port, and as the men sipped the heady liquid, they both began to relax.

'Do you remember when we first met?'

'In Helsinki. Of course I remember.'

'It was right after you had solved *The Mystery of the Ferry Crossing*. I had read about you in the newspaper and there you suddenly were, walking into my hotel lobby.'

'I was in need of a Watson . . .' Bell said. 'It is funny that you mention it. That case has been on my mind.'

'If I remember correctly, it was the poor relation who did it. Are you suggesting some minor character was involved? You don't suspect Dorcas, do you?'

'No, of course not.* I'm not sure what has put it into my mind,' said Bell. 'I have been thinking a lot about the past these days. Trying to find something that . . . Oh, I don't know. My mind is tired after all the interrogations.'

'I think we should have a small supper and then go to bed,' said Sacker. 'It will do you the world of good.'

He called over the landlady, who conjured up a big pot of bubbling stew and two glasses of red wine.

'I could get used to this,' said Sacker.

Bell was hungrier than he thought. Sometimes when he was working, he could forget to eat, forget to sleep, forget to do anything but focus on the matter at hand.

'So, which one of them did it?' Sacker asked. 'Which one of them is lying?'

'It could be more than one,' said Bell distractedly.

'An *Orient Express* situation?' asked Sacker excitedly.

'That's not what I meant. I just thought that there could be

---

* 'Servants – such as butlers, footmen, valets, game-keepers, cooks, and the like – must not be chosen by the author as the culprit. This is begging a noble question. It is a too easy solution. It is unsatisfactory, and makes the reader feel that his time has been wasted. The culprit must be a decidedly worth-while person – one that wouldn't ordinarily come under suspicion; for if the crime was the sordid work of a menial, the author would have had no business to embalm it in book-form.' S. S. Van Dine's 'Twenty Rules for Writing Detective Stories'

multiple lies here. Unrelated lies. A cover-up that isn't really covering up anything.'

Sacker was confused, as he often was.

'I can't believe that Abigail would have been involved. I mean, her own brother!'

'But you are forgetting, Sacker, the many crimes we have investigated that were committed by kin. You will recall *The Death in the Drain Pipe* or *The Mystery of Mr Plimpton's Good Hat*. Family can kill, and they will. Sometimes it is a madness. Sometimes a jealousy, a misunderstanding, an inheritance.'

'Oh, *The Death in the Drain Pipe*,' Sacker said wistfully. 'When I got my heart broken by that red-haired beauty. Do you think someone could rustle up a dame for me this time? I need a bit of fun.'

Soon, they retired to bed. Sacker fell immediately asleep, as was his way, but Bell had difficulty drifting off. Eventually, he gave up. He turned on the small lamp in his room and sat by his desk instead.

Bell circled around the idea of motive. His job was to disentangle the dynamics and find a way through the gorse. Crime-solving was not as difficult as people think. You just needed to push a little until people revealed something to you – this could be guilt or omission or some tension, some grinding between two lives. It was slow work, but when the revelation came, it would be a glorious relief. He had learned to be patient and to allow the revelations to find him.

He hadn't yet figured out the atmosphere of the grand house, hadn't yet settled on a narrative of how all these people interacted. He had seen a little of something between Abigail and Stephen that he would need to tease out further. It may well be that this had nothing to do with the death, but it was helpful to have the full picture of the inner lives of all the house guests.

Of course, Stephen was a suspect, but then again so was everyone at this stage. He had the opportunity, but what was his motive? That was the thing. Abigail got to the body first, but then, she was the client. An attempt at a double bluff? Not when the police had already declared it a suicide. Why would she draw attention to herself like this? And again, no apparent motive to think of. Barbara's position in all of this was still unclear, which immediately made Bell suspicious, but he had nothing concrete to go on. Declan with his gambling debts may have had a motive but he had the least opportunity of anyone. Then there was Margaret – who was still an enigma.

Bell had come to the end of it for now. He could do nothing more. He returned to his bed, turned off the lamp and slept fitfully for the rest of the night.

*

When he awoke in the morning, he made his toilet and then came downstairs to meet Sacker for breakfast.

'I have not slept on such a comfortable mattress in a long time,' said Sacker. 'I will have to ask the landlady where she bought it so that I can get one for my apartment. Did you sleep well?' Sacker asked, before remembering that Bell never slept well during a case. 'Oh, well, of course you wouldn't have.'

The landlady emerged and made polite enquiries of both

gentlemen. It was clear that she knew who Bell was but was trying to be coy about it. Bell had no interest in coyness. He just wanted information.

Sacker asked for some kippers and toast and Bell ordered some eggs and black coffee. When she returned with their order, Bell took the opportunity to act on his hunch.

'Thank you, we will need this food to build us up for the big day ahead.'

'Of course, sir. I hope you won't mind me asking, but are you that famous detective who's up at the big house? That terrible matter . . .'

'Yes,' said Bell. 'Do you know the family?'

'In a sense,' said the landlady. 'They're not the types of people who would be socializing with the likes of me, but I would see them around sometimes. The girl more often – very pleasant sort of person. I was very sorry for them after their parents died. My father used to do some work at the house, and he always said they were good people. Never had a bad word to say about them.'

'And what about Benjamin?' Bell asked.

'He wasn't here much. I remember him as a small boy but I suppose, funnily enough, I did see him on the day he died . . .' said the woman. Her eyes twinkled a little. Bell could see that she had been waiting eagerly to share this information with him.

'On the day he died? How so, madame?'

'He arrived with a woman and another man. They must have been coming from the city. He needed some oil for his car and my husband is the local mechanic so while he was waiting, I invited him in. He and the woman came inside out of the cold while the other man stood outside smoking. I don't like smoking inside. I have bad lungs.'

'Could you describe this woman for me?' asked Bell, and the landlady provided a rough description of Margaret.

'Ah, yes,' Bell said. 'Was there some information you wished to impart?'

'Well, the only thing,' said the landlady, 'and I don't like to gossip, but they were arguing a little. That woman wasn't happy with what he was telling her.'

'And what was it that he was saying?' asked Bell.

'I couldn't really hear. It was something like "it's been a long time; you should have moved on" and then also "it's my life – I can choose to spend time with whomever I want". That's all I heard, really. I couldn't hear very well. I had a bad cold over Christmas, and it has affected the hearing in my left ear. By the time my husband came back with the oil, the woman was looking very angry. He had to convince her to get back into the car. I hope I'm not speaking out of turn.'

'Of course not,' said Bell. 'You have been very helpful.'

The landlady left them to ponder what she had said. She looked a little pleased with herself.

'It seems Margaret wasn't quite as over the relationship as she let on,' said Sacker.

'It seems that way,' said Bell.

'And it confirms the relationship with Barbara,' said Sacker.

'Yes, I wonder . . .' said Bell. 'I wonder . . .'

The landlady came back to refill their coffee cups.

'Do you need a lift back to the big house?' she asked.

'We'll call a cab,' said Sacker.

'Oh, no need for that. My husband would be happy to drop you up.'

Bell smiled a little. It was clear that the woman and her husband were curious about what was going on. Their standing amongst the rest of the village would rise exponentially if they gathered any interesting information to share.

'That would be very kind, madame,' said Bell.

The landlady's husband helped carry their luggage to his car and then drove back up the winding rural roads to Yew Tree House.

'I hope my wife wasn't gossiping too much,' the man said.

'Oh no, not at all, sir. In fact, she was very helpful,' said Bell.

'I don't agree with gossiping. I believe in discretion. Especially now. I mean, it's not right to talk about the fact that they had to lay off two of their gardeners and make their remaining gardener part-time only. Or that they had stopped buying the expensive firewood from the village. It's not right to be telling tales.'

'Indeed,' said Bell.

*

Abigail's alarm goes off at 7 a.m. She says, 'Hey Siri, turn off', but nothing happens. She clears her throat, moistens her mouth, and repeats, 'Hey Siri, turn off', and her alarm immediately stops. She doesn't get out of bed. She can't. Well, that's not accurate. She could physically get out of bed, but her head is so heavy it feels as though movement would be impossible. Everything seems difficult. She goes through her to-do list in her head, and it is simple: she needs to have a shower and wash her hair, she needs to get dressed and do her skincare and her make-up and then dry her hair and straighten it. She needs to do her grocery shopping. The supermarket opens at 8 a.m. on Saturdays. Then, once she is back home, she will unpack the groceries and clean the bathroom before she has her breakfast and heads out the door. She tells herself that if she is out of the shower by 7.30 a.m. that will be fine. That means she can lay in bed just a little longer and right now it feels as though the whole concept of getting out of bed would bring an extreme level of pain that she would not be able to endure. Her brain is telling her that everything is bad, that she is bad, that staying in bed is bad but also getting out of bed would be bad too. Maybe if she just sleeps for a short while more – she is so tired – she will be able to get out of bed. But the next time she checks the time on her phone it is 8.01 a.m. She touches her hair, and it is greasy, and she realizes that it will be at least 9 a.m. before she gets to the supermarket now and that will be too late. There is no point. The day is ruined. She may as well stay in bed. This is just a bad day. Maybe tomorrow will be a better day. Tomorrow she will be better. Tomorrow she will complete her schedule and won't have this weight on her chest. Whatever she has to do today she will do tomorrow. She deserves this. Today will just be a write-off. She doesn't fall back asleep, but she drifts through sleepiness. By the time she does get out of bed it is 10.30 a.m. She has wasted so much of her day already. What's the point? She goes and has a shower and that makes her feel a little better and then a little worse at how easy it was. She dresses herself and does her skincare and dries her hair roughly. It is now 11.20 a.m. and half the day is gone. She feels rushed. She doesn't want to go grocery shopping now; she likes doing it in the early morning, so she moves that item on her to-do list. She could clean her bathroom, she supposes. She goes back downstairs and gathers up her cleaning supplies. She first puts away the shampoo bottle and conditioner bottle and shower gel that are in the basin of the shower. She gathers up all the towels and puts them in the washing machine. Then she does a cursory clean of the shower and toilet and sink. It is not properly clean, but she feels like she can tick it off her to-do list. It is 12 p.m., and she hasn't had anything to eat yet. She goes to her fridge and moves things around. There is no real food there, nothing she would want to eat. She goes to her food cupboard and does the same. And then the freezer. Nothing to eat, nothing to eat. She needs to plan her grocery list better. She could make something; she could walk to the local shop for supplies, but all of this feels like an immense effort. She doesn't want to go out to eat; that seems like too much pressure right now. She sits down in an armchair, gets her phone out and rechecks her to-do list. She won't be able to do any of this today. She moves it all to Sunday. But she needs to do something. She will check Instagram first. And then her email. And *The Guardian* app. And then Instagram again. And then back to her to-do list. She checks her list for the next week. She should go for a walk. She tries to get at least thirty minutes of exercise a day. She decides she will tidy her kitchen but after ten minutes she feels exhausted. She has done enough, she supposes.

Chapter Fourteen

THE RETURN OF THE POLICE

Abigail arrived at the library door to inform Bell that Detective Inspector Ferret had returned.

'Ah, he must have some important news,' said Bell. 'I wasn't expecting him until at least Chapter Eighteen.'

Out in the hallway, Ferret was waiting, hands in the pockets of his long brown trench coat, looking uncomfortable in the grand house.

'Ah, Inspector. Do you have news for us?'

'Could we speak somewhere private, Bell?'

Bell showed him into the library and shut the door behind them.

'Sorry for the cloak and dagger but we're trying to keep everything hush-hush,' Ferret said.

'Yes, of course. Is it about these thefts?'

'Yes, but between you and me, I'm not just here to investigate some piddling burglaries.'

'I did wonder,' said Bell, 'why a detective inspector would be out in the countryside looking for some run-of-the mill thieves!'

'Oh, these aren't any ordinary thieves, Bell. We've been trying to break up a jewellery smuggling ring with links to

Antwerp, and we believe that these thefts were carried out by that criminal organization. They seem to be in possession of a lot of information about the contents of stately homes. We've been hunting them across the country for the past year. But we're closing in on them now. They've gotten a little sloppy these last few burglaries. Soon, someone will slip up and then we'll have them.'

'How did you trace them here?'

'We were tipped off by someone on the inside. They're in our sights, Bell,' said Ferret.

'It does seem like an odd coincidence that this criminal gang would be in the area on the night that a murder takes place,' said Bell.

'I agree. As you know, I don't really like coincidences. Our intelligence suggests that the jewellery-smuggling ring hasn't moved on since that burglary four nights ago, which is unusual. And since you're investigating a murder, I was wondering whether you had uncovered anything in your investigations so far suggesting that this gang might have been involved?'

Bell felt the weight of the single gold earring in his inside pocket. He decided it wasn't time to show it to the inspector. He knew more than most how important it is to reveal clues gradually, in order to build tension. And anyway, it wasn't proof of anything yet.

'I have not seen any compelling evidence, though as you know, Abigail says she heard noises in the night. And if you stick around until Chapter Sixteen, I will soon speak with someone else who will say the same, though I cannot confirm the veracity of their claims as of yet. Also, my inspection of the rooms in the next chapter will show that a lot of expensive jewellery has remained in this house over the past day or two, not to mention the money contained in the safe and the paintings on the walls, all untouched.'

'Yes, well, like I told you,' said Ferret. 'There's an outside chance, but I just wanted to keep you informed. And, once again, I don't like coincidences.'

'Thank you very much, Inspector. If you hear anything else, then please do alert us.'

He walked Detective Inspector Ferret to the door and bid him farewell.

'What did the inspector have to say?' asked Abigail once he had gone.

'They have tracked a jewellery-smuggling ring to this area. He is keeping me updated in case it has anything to do with your brother's murder.'

'Oh my god,' said Abigail, genuinely shocked. 'Do the police think this ring murdered Benjamin?'

'They are gathering evidence, but right now it seems unlikely,' said Bell. He did not want to give her any false hope.

They were interrupted then by Stephen.

'I'm sorry,' he said. 'I was just wondering if you were hungry, Abigail? I don't think you've eaten all day.'

'No, no, I'm okay,' said Abigail.

'I think you should eat something,' Stephen said gently, taking her hand. 'C'mon, even just some tea and toast.' As he led her to the kitchen, Bell heard him joking, 'You'll have to show me how to use a kettle.'

*

The Garda is kind in a way that makes her hate him. He offers her tea, coffee, water, but she doesn't want anything. He tells a silly joke that makes her want to stand up and leave and never come back. It isn't his fault. It probably works on other people. But she doesn't feel like being placid and easy-going today. She has an excuse now. They can't call her a bitch for not smiling. 'Did your brother ever suffer from depression, anxiety, any diagnosed mental illness?' the Garda asks. The answer is an easy 'no' but that feels too simple. It wouldn't have explained anything, it wouldn't have helped, and yet 'yes' isn't true either and so Abigail says simply, 'I don't think so', because that seems like the closest to the truth right now. 'Did he have any money problems?' (She didn't know.) 'No.' 'Any relationship issues?' (That's a little complicated.) 'No.' 'Your parents . . . they are also deceased?' (An easy subject at last.) 'Yes, my mother sixteen years ago and my father nearly ten.' The Garda looks up. 'I'm very sorry about that. Do you have any close relatives?' 'An aunt. She lives not far from me.' 'That's good, that's good.' It sounds like he is reassuring himself more than anything. 'Could you set out in detail everything that happened on the thirty-first of December and the first of January?' he asks. She has repeated this story so many times over the last few weeks that she finds it easy to slip into the narrative, gone over it so often that it has taken on a specific shape and feel. The Garda just listens, occasionally taking notes. He interrupts her once or twice to ask about specific timings but that is it. He just allows her to say her piece. When she is finished, he thanks her, and it feels genuine. He tells her that if she needs anything she should call the station and ask for him. He has a very kind voice. He asks for the name of her liaison officer and when she tells him he replies that he is a good man who is very good at his job. 'You can lean on him if you need to,' he says. 'That's what he's there for.' She doesn't want to hate him, but she thinks if she never saw him again it would be too soon. They shake hands and she leaves the station. She walks to the bus stop but then keeps walking. And she doesn't put her earbuds in like she would normally, and she doesn't go over her to-do list in her head because there is no to-do list. She wonders where everyone else is headed: some going home as well, others just starting their working day, others still heading out for a midweek drink. Other lives just continue without you. That thought makes her feel dizzy and she has to stop and lean a hand against a wall for a moment. And then when she looks up, she suddenly sees him, standing with his back to her waiting for a green man. His hair, the slope of his shoulders . . . it is Benjamin. All the noise on the street is suddenly reduced to a thin metallic sound. A tightly wound ball of panic is lodged in her throat. Her skin fizzes. Abigail starts to walk towards him, bumping up against people she cannot see clearly. She nearly calls out his name, but she stops herself because she knows that it isn't him. It can't be. It isn't Benjamin. It isn't her brother. The man turns his face just slightly and she sees now that he is a much older man. And her panic is replaced by overwhelming sadness.

Chapter Fifteen

THE EVIDENCE OF THE GUESTS' ROOMS

Bell and Sacker joined the group in the drawing room. 'It is now time for me to inspect each of your bedrooms,' Bell declared.

'The police already did that,' said Cormac. 'And they didn't find anything of relevance.'

'I have a lot of respect for the police,' said Bell. 'They do an important job and I know some fine policemen, but they tend to overlook things. Especially when they already have their minds made up. They make mistakes. And of course, I have my methods.'

'Of course,' said Abigail. 'Would you like me to show you the way?'

As she led both Bell and Sacker upstairs, Bell paused briefly on the landing in front of the collection of shotguns and exclaimed a nearly imperceptible 'ah!' before continuing to the first floor.

Abigail explained the layout: 'Benjamin had the largest room and of course you know where that is. Directly across from him was Stephen in the yellow room and next door is the small box room where I slept. I gave my room to Cormac and Olivia as they are the only couple. I put Barbara into what we call the blue room and then Margaret was in here. That was where Declan would have stayed if he hadn't fallen asleep downstairs. But of course, all his belongings are there if that's what you are interested in.'

'Ah, very good, mademoiselle, I think we have the layout now. When we are finished, I will come and get you.' They waited until they couldn't hear her footsteps anymore.

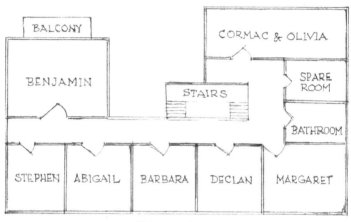

FIRST FLOOR

'Where do you want to begin?' Sacker asked.

'I think we will start with Cormac and Olivia's room.'

Cormac and Olivia's room faced the back of the house and had pleasant views of fields and trees. It was not particularly tidy. The bed hadn't been made and there were clothes strewn over it. Bell inspected quietly and methodically. He opened the wardrobe; he checked the chest of drawers. In the top drawer was a bottle of Clairol and a small bag of make-up.

'Very good of Abigail to give up her room. It must have been a bit of an annoyance for her to have to move all her things,' said Sacker.

'I think she tries to be the perfect hostess,' said Bell.

'Any smoking gun yet?' asked Sacker.

'You know my method,' said Bell. 'We need to allow things to rise to the surface.'

Bell then moved on to Margaret's room and Sacker followed. The room was orderly, as one might expect: a selection of evening gowns in the wardrobe, an empty perfume atomizer and some delicate silver jewellery on the dresser, and her other clothes neatly folded in the chest of drawers. Sacker watched as Bell surveyed every object

Next to that was Declan's room.

'He hasn't even bothered to unpack,' said Sacker. And indeed, all of Declan's clothes were still in his suitcase. The wardrobe was bare, as was the chest of drawers and of course the bed hadn't been slept in.

'Whose room is next?'

'Barbara.'

'Ah,' said Sacker. 'The temptress!'

Barbara's room was painted bright blue and had been kept neat and tidy by its occupant.

'What exactly are we looking for? Something racy?' Sacker asked as he gazed out the window at the gravel drive below.

'We are not looking for anything in particular. We are just seeing if the police missed anything. Some detail that might jump out at me.'

Bell opened the wardrobe and trailed a finger along the garments hung there: one fine evening dress, a travelling outfit, and a coat. Then he went to the chest of drawers. On top of it was a small jewellery box, some cold cream, a hairbrush, and some make-up. Bell gently opened the jewellery box and examined the contents.

'Ah,' he said. Sacker peered over his shoulder.

'Have you found something?' he asked.

'Not exactly,' Bell said. 'It is what I haven't found that is so interesting.'

'What the devil does that mean?'

Bell didn't answer. Instead, he closed the jewellery box and headed towards the door. Next, they inspected Abigail's room. A single bed was squashed into a corner and around it was stacked all of her belongings.

Bell rooted around for a while until he found a small jewellery box. Inside, he found a pair of diamond earrings, a jumble of chains and a pearly seashell.

Lastly, in Stephen's room they found a crumpled tuxedo on the floor by the bed, a glass of water on the bedside locker and a small date book which Bell leafed through. Sacker admired the mural before beginning to casually inspect the wardrobe.

'Were they planning on going shooting?' asked Sacker.

'Why do you ask that?'

'Oh, there's just some shooting clothes here: trousers, a vest, a nice jacket.'

'I suppose they could have been – the estate is large enough.'

Sacker took out the trousers and held them up. 'It's very nice. His own family's tweed, I suspect. Do you think there is something going on between the sister and the best friend?'

'They do seem very close.'

Bell had joined him. He quickly spotted something tucked

in at the back of the wardrobe and pulled out a pair of wrinkled brown trousers. Then he pushed back the clothes that were hanging up so that he could clearly see the wardrobe floor.

'You're onto something, I know it,' said Sacker, but Bell did not respond. That would have been too easy. He didn't want to give the game away yet. It was only Chapter Fifteen.

To: Everyone
From: Fred (HR)
Re: re: kitchen rules/food going missing
Date: 25 January 2023

Hi All,

Since my last email, there have been more complaints about people's food going missing from the fridge and also about the absolute state of the kitchen. This is a shared space and that also means shared responsibilities. I am also finding it hard to believe that after our last meeting about stealing food, this has continued to happen. I am frankly amazed. I will now reiterate the kitchen rules:

1. Always clean up after yourself. This includes cleaning plates, cups etc and replacing them in the correct storage space. It is not good enough to put them in the sink even if you say you are coming back later to do the washing. All washing-up needs to be done there and then. Also, please make sure that you clean up any spills on kitchen counters etc. There is a sweeping brush behind the door – use it.

2. Please put the milk back in the fridge the moment you are finished with it.

3. If there is food in the fridge or anywhere else in the kitchen marked with someone else's name, please

do not touch it. <u>No stealing food.</u> Since the meeting, there have been another three instances of food being stolen and so a CCTV camera will now be installed in the kitchen to deter this happening again. This is a serious matter. A lot of expense is being put into this. If someone is caught stealing a co-worker's food, a disciplinary hearing will commence.

4. Please refrain from bringing in any food that is particularly pungent, especially if you eat at your desk.

5. Also, while the coffee facilities are there for your use and enjoyment, please don't take the piss. This department is going through coffee capsules twice as fast as any other department. I know some people are taking them home. This is against the rules. Coffee is for consumption in the office only.

6. If you notice that the rubbish bin is full, please take the plastic bag to the big bin in the basement. Please do not just start placing rubbish on top of the kitchen bin.

7. Please wipe down the microwave after every use.

8. If you do store food in the fridge, please make sure you don't forget about it. Either eat it in time, take it home or throw it out. Please do not leave mouldy or gone-off food in the fridge.

And finally, please take pride in this space where we spend most of our waking hours and help make it a nicer and more pleasant place for us all to work in.

Chapter Sixteen

THE EVIDENCE OF THE ENGAGED COUPLE

B ell decided to take a walk by himself to clear his mind. He wasn't really one for a muddy tramp through fields, but he was quite happy to walk through manicured gardens, even if those surrounding Yew Tree House had a feel of faded glory about them. There was a rose garden and a covered walkway and apple trees and a walled vegetable garden, but Bell could spot the weeds and the untidy edges of the lawn. He wondered how one single gardener could ever take care of all of this.

Coming back around the side of the house, Bell met Cormac and Olivia. Olivia was wearing sunglasses that covered a large portion of her face.

'We needed to get out. Things are a little stifling inside right now,' explained Cormac.

'Exercise is good for the brain,' said Bell. He decided to take his opportunity. 'I have yet to ask you about your theories of what happened.'

'I know I shouldn't say this,' said Cormac, 'and please don't repeat it to Abigail, but I agree with the initial assessment of the police.'

'You believe that Benjamin took his own life?'

Cormac nodded sadly. 'Unfortunately, it seems like the most obvious solution.'

'That is surprising. You are the only person so far who believes that this is in fact suicide.'

'Well, it can be a difficult thing to admit,' said Cormac.

'Do you have any evidence for this? I mean, do you know something the rest don't?'

'Are you asking if I noticed any signs? Because the simple answer is no. This has come as a complete shock to me, but I can't just ignore the facts. The police have investigated, the doctor has examined the body. I am sure that in time you will come to the same conclusion yourself.'

'Well, we shall see. Do you –' Bell turned to Olivia – 'agree with your companion?'

'Oh, well,' said Olivia, a little flustered, 'I didn't know Benjamin that well. I suppose— It's just the door was locked. But I wouldn't like to speculate.'

'How long have you two been in a relationship?' Bell asked Olivia.

'Oh, we've been together for three years now,' answered Cormac. 'And engaged for just a couple of weeks, of course.'

'Yes, of course. Congratulations to the both of you. Will the wedding be happening soon?'

'We'll probably have a small ceremony sometime this year,' said Cormac, 'but obviously with what has happened—'

'I think everyone would enjoy a big party,' said Bell. 'And you, mademoiselle – I think that I detect a faint accent. Where are you from originally?'

'Oh, Olivia's from here,' Cormac said, smiling.

'And—' started Bell, but he was interrupted.

'Well, we'd better get back inside,' said Cormac. 'It's getting a little cold standing here.'

Cormac put his hand on the small of Olivia's back and started to manoeuvre her past Bell, but then he stopped.

'Before I forget,' said Cormac. 'I actually did hear something in the night. It slipped my mind to tell the police but with all this talk about jewel smuggling it came back to me.'

'How did you hear about that?' asked Bell.

'Stephen mentioned something. Isn't it true? Wasn't there a police officer here about it?'

'It is correct that Detective Inspector Ferret is investigating a series of burglaries nearby. What was it that you heard?'

'I heard someone outside, during the night,' Cormac said. 'Someone walking along the gravel. It woke me up but at the time I didn't think much of it.'

'Well, that is very interesting. Very interesting indeed. Did you also hear this sound?' Bell asked Olivia.

Cormac laughed. 'Olivia's a very heavy sleeper. The house could have fallen down, and she'd still be slumbering.'

Olivia smiled tightly.

'Are you still suffering after the party?' Bell asked her. Olivia and Cormac both seemed to be taken aback.

'What do you mean?' Olivia stammered.

'I mean your sunglasses – are you still feeling the effects of the party last night?' said Bell with a smile.

'Oh, yes, I understand,' Olivia said. 'I have a little migraine, that's all.'

'Ah, migraines. Yes, I suffer from them myself – you should go upstairs to rest.'

'Yes, yes,' she said. 'That's what I am planning on doing.'

Bell watched them retreat to the house, that feeling again of something just out of reach.

*

Benjamin came over to my house on Christmas Eve and left on Stephen's Day. We had breakfast on Christmas Day morning and unwrapped presents. We went for a walk before lunch. During the meal, we took a call from our aunt. It was a normal Christmas. Benjamin was in a good mood.

Benjamin came over to my house on Christmas Eve ~~and left on Stephen's Day~~. We alternate hosting Christmas, and this was my year. We opened a bottle of prosecco, had some party bites and watched some Christmas movies. Everything was normal. Nothing out of the ordinary happened. We had breakfast on Christmas Day morning and unwrapped presents. We went for a walk before lunch. It has become our tradition. Just a short one as a way of giving the day some structure. During lunch we FaceTimed our aunt, who spends every Christmas and New Year with friends in Germany. She is a retired language teacher: she summers in the south of France, Easters in Italy . . . We chatted for fifteen, twenty minutes. ~~During the meal, we took a call from our aunt~~. It was a normal Christmas. Benjamin was in a good mood.

~

Benjamin came over to my house on Christmas Eve. We alternate hosting Christmas, and this was my year. We opened a bottle of prosecco, had some party bites and watched some Christmas movies. Everything was normal. Nothing out of the ordinary happened. I went to bed a little after 11:30 p.m. Benjamin went to bed later – I heard him coming upstairs but I'm not exactly sure of the time. We had breakfast on Christmas Day morning and unwrapped presents. I got up as usual on Christmas Day and Benjamin got up maybe twenty or thirty minutes afterwards which gave me time to start making the coffee and heat up the pastries. I still get excited about opening Christmas presents. Benjamin could be grumpy in the mornings, but he soon warmed up because it was Christmas. We took our mugs of coffee and warm croissants into the sitting room where we leisurely unwrapped presents. He bought me a beautiful pair of earrings. We went for a walk before lunch. It has become our tradition. Just a short one as a way of giving the day some structure. We used to go and visit our parents' grave, but it messed with the day. It wasn't right. We go instead in the middle of summer when it is sunny and warm, and we bring bright flowers to put on the grave. During lunch we FaceTimed our aunt who spends every Christmas and New Year with friends in Germany. She is a retired language teacher: she summers in the south of France, Easters in Italy . . . We chatted for fifteen, twenty minutes. After lunch, we moved into the sitting room and ate trifle and had more wine and watched movies. We played a board game, we talked. Everything was fine. It was a normal Christmas. Benjamin was in a good mood.

~

Benjamin came over to my house on Christmas Eve. We alternate hosting Christmas, and this was my year. We opened a bottle of prosecco, had some party bites and watched some Christmas movies. Everything was normal. Nothing out of the ordinary happened. I went to bed a little after 11:30 p.m. Benjamin went to bed later— I heard him coming upstairs but I'm not exactly sure of the time. I got up as usual on Christmas Day and Benjamin got up maybe twenty or thirty minutes afterwards which gave me time to start making the coffee and heat up the pastries. I still get excited about opening Christmas presents. We do it together while sitting by the tree in my front room. Benjamin could be grumpy in the mornings, but he soon warmed up because it was Christmas. We took our mugs of coffee and warm croissants into the sitting room where we leisurely unwrapped presents. He bought me a beautiful pair of earrings. We went for a walk before lunch. It has become our tradition. Just a short one as a way of giving the day some structure. We walked in a loop from my house – past the primary school, past the closed coffee shop – and didn't meet anyone. Everyone was enjoying their Christmases behind their wreathed doors. We didn't talk about anything in particular – nothing important. Benjamin pointed out the perfect frost on the blades of grass in one field shaded by high trees. I told him about a neighbour's dog – it was nothing. Just a lot of early-morning barking. I had been irritated by it. I went on about it a bit too much. I remember the sound of our collective breath – that was the silence, I suppose. And then we started on the walk home. Everything was normal. We used to go and visit our parents' grave, but it messed with the day. It wasn't right. We go instead in the middle of summer when it is sunny and warm, and we bring bright flowers to put on the grave. <u>I always do Christmas lunch and Benjamin is in charge of dessert. This year he made a trifle. I went and changed my clothes and then I checked on the food. I don't know where Benjamin was during this time. When I came back to the kitchen, I called for him and he came out from the sitting room, I think. He was still dressed in his outdoor clothes, and I admonished him. He went to change.</u> During lunch we FaceTimed our aunt who spends every Christmas and New Year with friends in Germany. She is a retired language teacher: she summers in the south of France, Easters in Italy . . . We chatted for fifteen, twenty minutes. After lunch, we moved into the sitting room and ate trifle and had more wine and watched movies. We played a board game, we talked. Everything was fine. It was a normal Christmas. Benjamin was in a good mood.

~~Benjamin came over to my house on Christmas Eve. We alternate hosting Christmas, and this was my year. We opened a bottle of prosecco, had some party bites and watched some Christmas movies.~~ Everything was normal. ~~Nothing out of the ordinary happened. I went to bed a little after 11:30 p.m. Benjamin went to bed later – I heard him coming upstairs but I'm not exactly sure of the time. I got up as usual on Christmas Day and Benjamin got up maybe twenty or thirty minutes afterwards which gave me time to start making the coffee and heating up the pastries. We do it together while sitting by the tree in my front room. Benjamin could be grumpy in the mornings, but he soon warmed up because it was Christmas. We took our mugs of coffee and warm croissants into~~

the sitting room where we leisurely unwrapped presents. He bought me a beautiful pair of earrings. We went for a walk before lunch. It has become our tradition. Just a short one as a way of giving the day some structure. We walked in a loop from my house – past the primary school, past the closed coffee shop – and didn't meet anyone. Everyone was enjoying their Christmases behind their wreathed doors. We didn't talk about anything in particular – nothing important. Benjamin pointed out the perfect frost on the blades of grass in one field shaded by high trees. I told him about a neighbour's dog – it was nothing. Just a lot of early-morning barking. I had been irritated by it. I went on about it a bit too much. He didn't say anything. Did he react? Was he completely silent throughout? I remember the sound of our collective breath – that was the silence, I suppose. And then we started on the walk home. Everything was normal. We used to go and visit our parents' grave, but it messed with the day. It wasn't right. We go instead in the middle of summer when it is sunny and warm, and we bring bright flowers to put on the grave. I always do Christmas lunch and Benjamin is in charge of dessert. This year he made a trifle. I went and changed my clothes and then I checked on the food. I don't know where Benjamin was during this time. When I came back to the kitchen, I called for him and he came out from the sitting room, I think. He was still dressed in his outdoor clothes, and I admonished him. He went to change. During lunch we FaceTimed our aunt who spends every Christmas and New Year with friends in Germany. She is a retired language teacher: she summers in the south of France, Easters in Italy . . . We chatted for fifteen, twenty minutes. After lunch, we moved into the sitting

~~room and ate trifle and had more wine and watched movies.~~
~~We played a board game, we talked~~. Everything was fine. It
was a normal Christmas. ~~Benjamin was in a good mood.~~

Benjamin came over to my house on Christmas Eve.
Everything was normal. Nothing out of the ordinary hap-
pened. I went to bed a little after 11:30 p.m. Benjamin went
to bed later – I heard him coming upstairs but I'm not exactly
sure of the time. We had breakfast on Christmas Day morn-
ing and unwrapped presents. We went for a walk before
lunch. We didn't meet anyone. During lunch we FaceTimed
our aunt. After lunch, we moved into the sitting room and
ate trifle and had more wine and watched more movies. We
played a board game, we talked. That evening, we watched
Christmas movies. It was a normal Christmas. Benjamin was
in a good mood. He went home on Stephen's Day.

Chapter Seventeen

A RECITATION OF THE FACTS

'Let us go over the facts,' declared Bell, 'or at least those facts which are indisputable. A man is found dead behind a locked door the morning after a New Year's Eve party. It also happens to be his birthday. The door to the balcony is unlocked. The broken alarm clock says half past three. A single earring is found which no one has claimed. Everyone besides Barbara and Olivia have known each other for many years. On one hand it seems unlikely that Benjamin would be murdered by a close friend but on the other hand resentment breeds over time. Declan says he was downstairs all night asleep except for his visit to the bathroom. His night-time ramble was heard by Barbara who was awoken by his steps. He is in debt. Benjamin has cut him off. No one else admits to leaving their rooms in the night. Stephen had an argument with Benjamin the afternoon before the party, and it was he who discovered that the door was locked. Cormac tries to lay the blame on an outsider – and perhaps he is correct. Given the balcony door was unlocked, in Chapter Twenty-Two we should check whether it is possible to scale the wall outside. Cormac is reluctant to allow Olivia to speak to me. However, neither have, as far as I can tell, a motive for Benjamin's murder. The innkeeper overheard an argument between Margaret and Benjamin, and Margaret herself is suspicious of Barbara and has tried to pin the blame on her – that odd phone call. Barbara is hiding something. Was she having an affair with her employer? Does she know something about his financial losses? In fact, is anyone aware that Benjamin – and indeed Abigail – are in a precarious financial state? There is something about this case, Sacker, that I can't quite grasp hold of. There are nearly too many clues.'

'Well, let's make it a little easier for ourselves then,' said Sacker as he rose from his armchair in the corner of the library and retrieved the battered paperback from his jacket pocket. He started to turn the pages. 'Now let's see, let's see. Oh, look at this,' he said, and he began to read. 'On page 34, in the Cast of Characters: Margaret still wears her engagement ring hidden around her neck – that's very interesting! And a clear motive.'

Bell looked somewhat unimpressed, but Sacker continued reading regardless.

'And Olivia was a champion gymnast. I would never have thought it . . .' Sacker said. He skipped on a few pages and proceeded to narrate: *The stupid friend of the detective, the Watson, must not conceal any thoughts which pass through his mind; his intelligence must be slightly, but very slightly, below that of the average reader . . . he exists for the purpose of letting the reader have a sparring partner, as it were, against whom he can pit his brains. "I may have been a fool," he says to himself as he puts the book down, "but at least I wasn't such a doddering fool as poor old Watson."*

Sacker looked up from the book somewhat appalled.

'I say, that seems awfully unfair.'

'Don't take it personally,' said Bell.

'It's a little difficult not to,' grumbled Sacker as he flicked on a couple of pages. 'Ah here's something else. On page 73, when you interviewed Dorcas, and she accused Declan of stealing the gardener's screwdriver? Is that a clue?' he asked. 'Did someone remove the hinges of the door, kill Benjamin and then put the door back into place without disturbing the lock?'

'The hinges need to be on the outside of the door for that trick to work,' said Bell.

Sacker looked disappointed. He hoped that one day he would be able to solve a mystery all on his own. 'You know, we could just skip forward a couple of chapters and find the solution, right?' he said, flicking idly through the pages of the book.

'Oh no, don't ruin things, Sacker. The solution is only as satisfying as the build-up. Put that away.'

'At least let us use the cluefinder, Bell,' said Sacker, and he flicked to the back pages. He read: '*On page 53, Bell experiences an odd feeling of familiarity overtaking him, he feels "a sense that he was being transported back in time, some rustle of a memory that he couldn't grasp hold of quickly enough before it receded". This feeling reappears on page 144 – 'that feeling again of something just out of reach'. He seems repeatedly haunted by the past throughout the book, including when on page 119 he speaks to Sacker* (Oh! That's me!) *about the first time they met and Bell's first case* The Mystery of the Ferry Crossing. *On page 98, he complains about feeling nostalgic. Bell is experiencing that unusual feeling of déjà-vu: a face from his past has re—*'

But Bell stopped him. 'Sacker, please help me with something,' he said. 'Could you go without anyone seeing you into the small office and put a call through to Freeman, Wills, Croft & Associates for me. You should be able to get the number from the address book on the desk.'

'Yes, of course,' said Sacker. 'It will be as though I was invisible.'

Once the library door had closed behind him, Bell took a glance at the battered paperback but resisted the temptation. Soon, Sacker returned.

'Bell, I have managed to get a hold of someone in the office. Because of the holidays there is only a junior lawyer available,' he said. 'I hope this will be sufficient.'

'Ah yes, I am sure he will be able to answer my questions,' said Bell.

In the office, Bell took a seat and introduced himself to the young man on the other end of the line.

'Thank you so much for your help with this,' said Bell. 'I have one simple request: who is or indeed who *are* the beneficiaries of Benjamin's estate?'

Bell could hear the turning of pages.

'I am so sorry that I am not better prepared,' the young man said. 'I am just a junior associate.'

The detective assured him that he was doing fine.

'So,' the young man cleared his voice, 'the house and all its contents go to Abigail, the deceased's sister. As does the business and most of the money. There is a fair amount in a bank account which has been willed to a friend of the deceased's named Declan and several small sums which have been left to members of staff. Everything looks relatively simple.'

'That is very good. What is the date of that will?' Bell asked. More shuffling of papers.

'This will was made five years ago.'

'Ah,' said Bell, 'and please tell me, has Benjamin approached you about redrafting his will lately?'

'No,' the young man said. 'There are no records of him contacting the office. We haven't heard from him in months.'

'Thank you very much for all your help,' said Bell, and he rang off.

*

The restaurant is busy for a Wednesday evening. Abigail watches as the strangers around her continue with their lives indifferently. As if nothing has happened. As if everything is just the same. She wants to scream. She wants them all to feel pain the way that she does. She wants them to notice. Frances is complaining to her. Last year, she had agreed to be a bridesmaid in their mutual friend's wedding and is now regretting it. 'We're all barrelling towards thirty, for god's sake,' she is saying. 'She shouldn't even be having bridesmaids. It's embarrassing.' Why did you say yes, Abigail wants to ask, but doesn't. 'The dress is terrible. They didn't even have my size in the shop, so they had to send away for it and I'm dreading its arrival. It's so flimsy. The material is so cheap. And the colour . . . It's not just that it doesn't suit me . . . it doesn't suit any of us. Maybe it suits Kelly but that's just because she's thin. I mean it doesn't really *suit* her. Wait, hold on, I'll show you a picture of it . . . I have it here somewhere in my phone . . . you'll see . . . wait, no that's not it . . . erm, it's something . . . no hold on . . . god, my entire phone is just bridesmaid dresses . . . I thought I had it. I'll look for it later. But just think of a purple knee-length bridesmaid dress and that's it . . .' Frances pauses to take a sip of wine and to smear ricotta on her crostini. 'All these dresses are so outrageously expensive. I would have found a better dress if she had just handed over the search to me. I mean, I will never wear this again. It's such a waste. And for weeks I kept posting nice dresses to the WhatsApp group to see if we could get one of those instead, but it was like yelling at the moon. I would get no response, or the response would be days later, or it'd be like "yeah it's not the correct shade of lavender though" and she never once got back to me. I mean, it's so frustrating . . .' *My brother's dead*, Abigail thinks silently. *My brother's dead.* '. . . I spent my entire Saturday trying on dresses. What a waste of time. And I have to take two days off work for the wedding and the next day – the Saturday – will be a complete wash-out as well. And the worst thing is that she is so ungrateful. I wouldn't mind it so much if she said thank you every so often and acknowledged all the work that I'm putting into this but . . . oh I haven't told you about the hen do yet. That's another day off work and my entire weekend gone. And I know that I'll be running around doing everything as usual . . .' Abigail runs her hand across the edge of the table. Back and forth. Back and forth. *My brother's dead. My brother's dead.* '. . . and I was saying all of this to Matt, and he was like "just chill out, it's not that big of a deal, it's not even that important, why are you making such a fuss, blah blah blah" and I thought, *Well, that's typical.* That's what all men think because their view of a wedding is maybe a stag do or whatever but besides that they get a suit and then they turn up on the day. Weddings for them start about three months before the date whereas for us the moment that ring goes on you're getting emails and you're in a WhatsApp group and you've got a dress fitting and a night out for this and a night out for that and the meetings about the hen do and then there's the week of the wedding itself and make-up trials and on the day you're running around after the bride. It's free labour is what it is. And all they have to do is turn up in a suit that they probably just rented and enjoy the party. And he's telling me not to worry, that it will be all right on the day. The dress will look fine. You're beautiful. Blah blah blah . . .' A waiter comes and switches out their jug of water for a fresh one. Abigail pours herself a glass. It is cold and it feels good going down her throat. *My brother's dead. My brother's dead.* '. . . I would never do this to her. That's the thing. When I get married, I'll be like . . . actually, no, I won't even have bridesmaids, it's ridiculous. I'm too old for this. And I'll organize my own hen do, and people can wear whatever they want, or I'll just elope. I mean, that's the easiest way of dealing with it. I hate the idea of everyone spending money like that. I've spent, let me see . . . huh, so far . . . I think I've spent three hundred euro and that's just the beginning of it. There's a thing at her mother's house the week of the wedding and we have to bring a present to that and also, it's like a potluck thing so everyone has to bring food. So that's more time and money . . .' She shovels fennel salami into her mouth. Abigail has barely touched her plate. She has no appetite these days, but she is amazed how well she feels without eating. She doesn't even feel light-headed. Maybe she doesn't need food. *My brother's dead. My brother's dead.* '. . . and then the most annoying thing. Of course. Everything happens at once . . .' *My brother's face.* '. . . I have the NCT at the end of the month, so I bring my car for its annual service. I know a couple of things need to be done: the back wheels and there's a light on the dash . . .' *My brother's hands.* '. . . So, I thought I had a rough idea of how much it would cost but then I get a phone call, and it turns out there's all sorts of things wrong . . .' *My brother's eyes.* '. . . I thought the light on the dash was a sensor because it usually is but actually it's this whole . . . I don't even know what he was calling it and there's a problem with . . .' *My brother. My brother. My brother.*

Chapter Eighteen

A SECOND INTERVIEW WITH BARBARA

In the hallway, Bell and Sacker were interrupted by Barbara coming down the stairs. She began to apologize but Bell stopped her.

'I am so sorry to derail you, but a small piece of evidence has come to light,' he said.

Bell thought he saw a flicker of fear in Barbara's face as he held out the single gold earring.

'By any chance, is this your earring?'

Barbara took it from his outstretched palm and examined it. 'Oh, why yes, it is. Oh, thank you. I thought it was lost for ever.'

'It was found in Benjamin's room,' said Bell.

'In Benjamin's room?' echoed Barbara, amazed.

'Do you have any idea how it might have gotten there?' asked Bell.

'No, I mean – let me see – I suppose I must have dropped it when Benjamin invited me in before dinner to see the view from the balcony. I must have lost it then.'

'You were not in the room again, mademoiselle?' asked Bell.

'No, I was not,' said Barbara, looking him straight in the eye.

'It was found in Benjamin's pyjama pocket. Do you know how it might have gotten in there?'

Barbara looked confused. If she was lying, she was an excellent actress.

'No,' she said. 'I mean, he must have picked it up. I must have dropped it and he must have picked it up and put it in his pocket. That's the only thing that makes sense.'

'Yes, that is the only thing that makes sense,' said Bell.

*

'What was all that about?' asked Sacker. 'So what if it was her earring? All it proves is that they were having an affair.'

'Once again Sacker,' said Bell, 'you are completely—'

A noise interrupted him, and they both turned. Margaret was standing near the door to the drawing room. She had just emitted a short sharp cry. Her eyes were wide, her lips a thin line. Her hand was gripping the door frame. Gone was the Margaret who was cool, calm and collected.

'Is something wrong, mademoiselle?' Bell asked her. She didn't seem to hear him. 'Mademoiselle . . . ?' Bell repeated, walking towards her.

'Please, just leave me alone.' She stepped back from him.

He thought he could see the beginning of a tear in her eye.

'Of course,' Bell said, 'just one thing . . .'

He leaned forward and with his index finger he pulled at the gold chain around her neck until it was revealed in its entirety. On the end of it was a diamond ring.

'What a beautiful engagement ring. I can see why you held on to it.'

Margaret pushed Bell's hand away violently.

'Don't touch me, you foul man.'

She stuffed the necklace back under her dress, turned swiftly and rushed upstairs.

'Risky move,' said Sacker, 'but she obviously still holds a flame for the late departed Benjamin.'

'Yes, it does seem that way,' Bell said thoughtfully.

*

The meeting room is stuffy, so Abigail goes around and opens all the windows. She breathes in the fresh air deeply and puts her hand outside to cool down. *My brother's dead*, she thinks. *My brother's dead*. She waits there for the others, who pile in one by one. They say hello to her and throw their files down on the table. *My brother's dead my brother's dead my brother's dead*. Someone comes in with a phone to their ear. 'Yeah, yeah but the thing is . . . yeah yeah . . .' He goes around and closes all the windows without asking. *My brother's dead my brother's dead my brother's dead my brother's dead*. Some more people come in, obviously tired and hungover from post-work drinks the night before. *My brother's dead my brother's dead my brother's dead my brother's dead my brother's dead*. Eventually, the meeting starts only twelve minutes behind schedule. 'Welcome everybody . . . are we all settled? Okay. I just want to see if I can turn this thing on here . . . wait . . .' *My brother's dead my brother's dead my brother's dead my brother's dead my brother's dead*. 'Before we begin,' says the man on the phone, 'I have to leave at one thirty for a lunch and learn. I'll just slip out quietly, but we should probably start discussing next quarter just so I'm here for that. In case anyone has any questions. Otherwise, you can just email me later . . .' *My brother's dead my brother's dead my brother's dead my brother's dead my brother's dead.* 'Okay, so that's plugged into that. And that's plugged into that. And now the light is flashing which means we have to wait until, okay now the light is solid so . . . this is switched on and . . . it should just turn on. Oh, there we go!' *My brother's dead my brother's dead my brother's dead my brother's dead my brother's dead my brother's dead my brother's dead my brother's dead my brother's dead my brother's dead my brother's dead my brother's dead my brother's dead my brother's dead my brother's dead my brother's dead.* 'Abigail, could you please update us on your project? Have you received the final budget?' 'We had a little delay getting the contracts back *my brother's dead my brother's dead my brother's dead my brother's dead my brother's dead my brother's dead my brother's dead my brother's dead my brother's dead my brother's dead my brother's dead my brother's dead my brother's dead my brother's dead* we finally have those figures in and I'm waiting for approval which will happen this week *my brother's dead my brother's dead my brother's dead my brother's dead my brother's dead my brother's dead my brother's dead my brother's dead my brother's dead my brother's dead my brother's dead my brother's dead my brother's dead my brother's dead my brother's dead my brother's dead* but I think that we'll be able to keep to our deadline.' 'And Nathan, what's happening with . . .'

Chapter Nineteen

A VISIT FROM A PSYCHIC

Suddenly, there was a familiar screeching of car brakes from outside and Abigail appeared in the entrance hall.

'That must be my aunt,' she said.

'I thought she was staying with friends,' said Bell. 'Has she changed her mind?'

Abigail went outside to greet her and find out what was going on.

The aunt had arrived with an unusual woman in tow. This woman was tall – over six feet – and wore a glittery ankle-length red dress. She spoke with an accent Bell couldn't quite place – maybe Hungarian?

'This is Anastasia,' said the aunt. 'I had her brought up from the city at short notice. She is my personal psychic. She's here to help you and poor Benjamin.'

Abigail tried to find words to politely decline the offer, but it was difficult with Anastasia standing there sparkling over her.

'Maybe another time,' said Abigail eventually.

'Oh no,' said the aunt. 'It has to be now. While everything is still fresh. The nearer to the death, the closer Anastasia can get to the truth. She is a wonder. She can perform exorcisms too. She rid the Wimseys of all their ghosts and now their house hasn't been flooded in over two months.'

'Take me to the place of death,' intoned Anastasia. Abigail shook her head vehemently, but her aunt pushed past her into the entrance hall.

'Oh dear, can't you see – she needs to be in Benjamin's room in order to sense the spirits.'

'No, she doesn't,' said Abigail, hurrying after the psychic, who had strode across the entrance hall and was making her way up the stairs.

'Gather the household,' Anastasia intoned from the landing above. Abigail was left standing on the first step, her hand clinging to the banister to keep her upright. Her eyes were closed as she tried to steady herself.

'Will I gather the household?' asked the butler discreetly.

'I suppose you should,' Abigail said, and she started slowly to make her way up the stairs after her aunt and the psychic.

*

This was very much not Bell's thing. He didn't like clairvoyants or psychics or anything smacking of the supernatural. It had become more of a fad in recent years to the point that even the police used them sometimes, but Bell's world was very much of the material kind. It was rooted in facts and hard evidence. He could see that this was also not Abigail's thing. She looked very pale.

Anastasia was waving her arms about and chanting a mantra. The aunt looked on solemnly while Abigail squirmed in the doorway.

'Come into the room,' her aunt insisted. Abigail hesitated but then stepped inside. The clairvoyant sat suddenly on the bed where the body had been, and Abigail flinched.

'Something terrible has happened here.'

'Well, we know that,' said Cormac exasperatedly.

The aunt shushed him. The clairvoyant had her eyes closed.

'I can sense something. Wait, hold on. It's very strong. I'm finding it difficult to control . . . wait, okay, here now. Yes, yes, I see him . . .'

'Is it Benjamin?' asked the aunt.

Bell watched from across the room as Abigail's face contorted into a series of contradictory expressions. He couldn't imagine what she was going through.

'He's trying to tell me something . . . Wait, hold on. Yes, yes, I see. Oh – he's saying that he was murdered. He is asking us to avenge his death. He wants us to bring his killer to justice.'

'Who?' blurted out Abigail. 'Who is the murderer?'

'Oh, hold on, he's saying a name but . . . he's getting fuzzy. Wait, I'm seeing something, a shadow – it isn't clear. There is something – it's pulling him away from me. I'm trying to hold on but I—'

And then the clairvoyant collapsed backwards onto the bed.

'Go to her,' said the aunt. 'Help her.'

Stephen and Declan gently propped the clairvoyant up by the arms and she hazily opened her eyes.

'Wha-at happened?' she asked dreamily.

'Do you not remember?' asked Margaret.

'Oh, Anastasia can never remember what happens when she returns from the spirit world,' explained the aunt.

'That's convenient,' said Cormac quietly.

'We should bring her downstairs and get her a stiff drink. She'll need it before the car journey back to the Mallowans.'

Stephen and Declan reluctantly helped the clairvoyant down the stairs. The aunt followed with Abigail and the others behind her.

'That seemed like a phenomenal waste of time,' said Cormac.

'This is very much a side show,' agreed Bell.

*

Since her last visit, the aunt's feelings towards Bell had changed considerably. She had gone back to the Mallowans and told them about the funny little man who was investigating her nephew's death and was then informed by her hosts that he was in fact a very famous detective.

'I hadn't realized,' she said, 'that you were *the* Auguste Bell. I think you know my friends the Westmacotts – they live just outside of St Mary Mead. You helped them out a couple of years ago.'

Bell remembered them very well. The Westmacotts were an elderly couple who lived in a large house in the countryside. Their maid had ended up dead and an autopsy had revealed that she had been pregnant. A lot of idle village gossip posited that Mr Westmacott was the father of the unborn child and that he had killed her rather than come clean to his wife. The local police had been unable to solve the matter and so Bell was drafted in. It was a neighbour who did it, if he remembered correctly, though he hadn't been the father of the child. He had been jealous of the maid's relationship with a musician and had killed her in a rage of passion.

'It is time, I think,' said Bell, turning to Sacker, 'for us to retire once more to the inn.'

'An inn!' Abigail's aunt declared. 'I won't hear of it. You will come and stay with me at the Mallowans.'

'Oh,' said Bell. 'We couldn't intrude.' Though he wasn't really putting up a fight – he thought the neighbours might have some valuable clues to share.

'Don't be ridiculous. Just get your things and jump into my car,' said the aunt.

Bell and Sacker didn't need to be told twice. Bell gathered up his valise and Sacker went to collect his small brown suitcase and they placed their items in the boot of the car. Bell sat up front with the aunt – Sacker wanted to become better acquainted with the clairvoyant, who had tumbled into the back seat.

'You know I've always loved tall women,' Sacker was saying to the clairvoyant as the car eased down the driveway. 'What's your name again?'

Soon they were tearing down country roads at death-defying speeds. Abigail's aunt drove a little sports car and even though it was winter she had the top down. Bell pulled his scarf closer to him as the car veered around corners at an unrelenting pace. The aunt talked the whole time, though most of her words were caught by the wind. Bell held on to his hat and just hoped for the best. Sacker was now in deep discussion with the clairvoyant in the back seat. The wind whipped around them, and he had to lean in very closely so that they could hear each other. Sacker was an awful flirt.

About twelve minutes later, they arrived at the house belonging to the Mallowans – a grand mansion that frankly dwarfed Yew Tree House. Bell's legs were shaking as he walked towards the front door, where the butler came to greet them.

'Do you have any luggage?' he asked.

Abigail's aunt pushed her way through to the front hall and started calling for the man and lady of the house to come and join them. She wanted to show off her famous companion. The Mallowans soon assembled in the front hall: Lord and Lady Mallowan, their daughter Clarissa – well known on the horse circuit and tipped for the Olympics next year – their son Freddie – well known on the social scene for his scandalous parties – and their two fox terriers, Tommy and Tuppence. Bell was pushed towards them and shook hands with everybody.

'Thank you so much for allowing us to stay tonight,' said Bell.

'It's our honour to have a famous detective visit,' said Lady Mallowan.

'Oh god, wouldn't it be marvellous if there was a murder in the night,' said Freddie.

'Don't say that,' said Clarissa, who was a little bit more sensible than her brother.

Sacker entered behind Bell, arm in arm with the clairvoyant.

'I wonder if someone could help Anastasia to a quiet room. She's had quite the day,' said Sacker.

'Oh, it's so nice to have a man to look after me,' said the clairvoyant, her staccato voice reverberating around the grand hall. Bell saw Clarissa raise her eyes to the ceiling. Lady Mallowan called for a maid, who led the clairvoyant upstairs to her bedroom.

'We have a full house,' said Clarissa.

'Yes, isn't it nice,' said her mother. 'Like the old days.'

After the guests had a short rest and a chance to freshen up, the household gathered in the library for drinks and small talk before they were led into the dining room, where they were served a delicious meal of cucumber soup, salmon, pork chops and fruit pudding.

'Tell us about your favourite murder,' said Freddie.

'Oh, don't annoy Mr Bell during his dinner,' said Lord Mallowan. 'You can ask those questions in the drawing room later when we are having our drinks.'

'Yes, I don't want to talk murder over dinner,' said Clarissa.

'Oh, how boring!' said Freddie.

Sacker had magically found himself sitting next to the clairvoyant, who it turned out barely ate anything, and so he finished most of her dishes for her.

'Oh, you have such a big appetite,' the clairvoyant whimpered.

Bell should have expected this. The clairvoyant was exactly Sacker's type: pretty, vaguely foreign and a bit of a dolt. Bell half-expected him to be engaged by the end of the book but there would be no wedding. There never was.

'Did you know Benjamin at all?' Bell asked his hosts.

'We knew his parents, of course,' said Lord Mallowan. 'Fine people, but we don't know the children very well.'

'They keep to themselves,' said Freddie. 'Not really my crowd. They're a little conservative, I think. A little staid.'

'Freddie,' admonished Lady Mallowan.

'I went to school for a year or two with Abigail before she was sent abroad. She seemed okay. She did well in school and all that, but she was . . . unexceptional,' said Clarissa. 'Still a terrible thing to happen to her. And it really was murder?'

'That is what I am here to discover,' said Bell.

'I thought we weren't supposed to talk murder over the dinner table,' said Freddie reproachfully.

'This is different,' said Clarissa. 'This is the murder of someone we know.'

'Well, it's always different when the favourite brings it up,' said Freddie.

'Didn't he come to one of your parties – the one with the under-the-sea theme?' asked Lady Mallowan, hoping to avert a row in front of the guests.

Freddie thought a little. 'Oh, that's right. I invited him as usual, expecting him not to attend, but then he came by. Such a surprise!'

'He didn't come to the party,' said Lord Mallowan between bites of food. 'He came to speak to me.'

'What did he wish to speak to you about?' asked Bell.

'He was looking for a loan of money,' he replied quietly.

'How long ago was this?' Bell asked.

'It was –' Lord Mallowan glanced at his wife – 'two months ago.'

'And did you give him the money?' Bell asked.

'No. Well, I would have. I told him that we would meet again in the New Year and discuss things in full. I was thinking of buying some of his farmland. That would have solved problems for both of us, but now, well, it doesn't matter anymore.'

'Was he in financial difficulties?'

'That's the impression I got. He is a young man and of course he was putting a good face on things but I'm sure it would have hurt him to sell some of his father's land,' said Lord Mallowan.

After dinner they retired to the drawing room. It turned out that Lady Mallowan was quite political, and Bell was happy to chat and debate with her. Freddie played some piano and sang for them. He was actually rather good.

'You know we've never had a clairvoyant stay before,' said Freddie. 'We've had all sorts of royalty and lords and ladies and even an actress or two, but never a clairvoyant.'

'What is it that you do, exactly?' asked Clarissa sceptically.

'Oh well, it's a little too complicated to explain properly,' said the clairvoyant. 'I reach into the other world – it's a place not unlike limbo, where souls are stuck. And I, well, reach out there or indeed the person reaches out to me, and we have a connection. I never remember what happens exactly but that's what it feels like. I search through a shadowy land until I find someone, or they find me. They are stuck, you see. And they need for something to happen before they can move on to the other world entirely.'

'What did Benjamin have to say? I mean, that's why you were up at the house,' said Freddie.

'Oh, well –' the clairvoyant looked to Sacker – 'see, that's the thing. I don't remember. I never remember what is said to me. It takes up so much of my energy, you see.'

'I can tell you that Benjamin was seeking justice for his own murder,' said Sacker.

'So, he *was* murdered then,' said Freddie eagerly.

'Don't look so excited, Freddie,' said Lady Mallowan. 'It's unbecoming.'

'Oh, god, but it is a bit of excitement at last. Nothing fun ever happens here,' exclaimed Freddie.

'I wouldn't describe a sudden death as fun,' said Clarissa coolly.

'Yes, well, fun for you is ponies and daffodils and things like that.'

Soon after, finding he was tired, Bell decided to retire to his room. Of course, as soon as he was under the covers, he was wide awake again. He was still awake when the others came up to bed – he heard their creaking footsteps on the floorboards and their giggling whispers.

Bell tossed and turned for the rest of the night, and arose the next morning feeling groggy and momentarily confused to find himself in a different country house.

He and Sacker were treated to an elaborate breakfast in the large hall before being driven back to Yew Tree House. Abigail's aunt was still in bed, so they could not say goodbye, but Sacker theatrically kissed the hand of the clairvoyant as they departed.

'I'm going to marry her, Bell,' said Sacker.

'Won't you ever choose a suitable woman?' asked Bell.

'Don't you like her?'

'It has nothing to do with *like*,' Bell said. 'It's just that we both know that this won't work out.'

Sacker looked hurt.

'But this is it. She's the one,' he said reproachfully.

'That's what you said about that woman in Antigua and the Irish woman-pirate and that lady who was part of that gang in Boston,' said Bell. 'You're always falling in and out of love.'

'Not this time.' Sacker shook his head vehemently. 'This time it's for real.'

Bell ignored him. The gates to Yew Tree House had come into view and he had more important things to think about.

*

Clara had always been a bit of a gossip and Abigail had learned early on to stay out of her way. If she got any information about you at all she would run with it. One weekend, she had passed Abigail in the street holding hands with her then-boyfriend and by Monday morning the whole office knew she was in a relationship. Clara had breezed past just before lunchtime saying, 'good-looking boyfriend you have there', as if she had caught Abigail having a salacious affair. 'How tall is he? Six two? What's his name? I have to say, I thought you were a lesbian . . . I nearly introduced you to my cousin . . .' Abigail hadn't made a complaint then. She knew it would sound small and petty and she didn't want to get a reputation as someone who couldn't just deal with things like this on her own. But she never liked the idea that people were talking about her. Now Clara wants to buy her a coffee and won't take no for an answer. Abigail tries to make excuses: she has work to do, she isn't a big coffee drinker, maybe later, but it becomes impossible to avoid her. They meet at the coffee kiosk outside of their office building. It's quite warm, so they sit outside. 'How are you doing?' asks Clara. Abigail hates this question; there is no good way to answer it. 'Oh, I'm fine,' she says. A lie. 'It must be so difficult for you. I can't imagine. You know I had a tough time with my mother dying the year before last and when I heard about . . .' This sort of thing happens to Abigail all the time now. People identify a certain type of sadness in her, and they see it as a sign to use her as a receptacle for all the bad things that have happened to them. '. . . it really triggered something in me. You know? I thought I was okay. I thought I was coping but I wasn't. And I had to admit that to myself. And then when you came back to work – god, every time I see you, I feel so sad . . .' And then there are the people who try to wallow in her sadness alongside her. People who want her to stay down in her hole while they climb in after her. People who tell her confidently that she will never get over this or that everything happens for a reason. Abigail doesn't know how much more she can take. She is feeling very full of everyone's sadness and anger and regret. Someday she will topple over, or it will just burst out of her. '. . . so I go for a walk every morning because I've read that being close to nature is one of the best things you can . . .' Abigail gets so much advice now. She knows way too much about supplements and exercise and David Hume. 'And were you the one who found him?' Clara asks, eyes wide. 'Yes,' says Abigail. 'That must have been so difficult for you,' says her colleague, bathing in it. 'And what about your parents? They must be having such a difficult time. I mean to lose your child like that . . .' 'Both my parents are dead,' Abigail says. Clara's eyes light up. 'Oh, so you're all alone,' she says. 'Oh my god, you must be so devastated.' Abigail doesn't like the way she says *alone*. It sounds smug. She isn't sympathising, she is lording it over her. 'Do you have any family at all?' asks Clara. 'I have an aunt,' Abigail says coolly. 'Oh, well at least that's something but to lose both of your parents and then your brother. God, how do you go on?' Abigail doesn't respond. 'Did your parents die in a car accident?' 'No,' says Abigail. Clara pauses, presumably waiting for more, but it doesn't come. Even she can't find a way of asking for specifics. Abigail knows that this evening Clara will go home to her husband and say, 'Oh my god this poor girl at work! She's an orphan and her brother has just killed himself. Don't some people have terrible lives.' It makes Abigail feel very small.

*

She decides to send an email to HR. Really, it is just a simple request to be left alone. She is emotionally drained at the end of each working day, and she needs a break. The HR person agrees with her of course, I mean how could he not? Though he also tries to justify other people's actions by explaining to her that people mean well, that they all care for her, but that people sometimes don't say the right thing. Abigail doesn't need to hear that most people can't deal with grief. She knows that. But she wants her feelings to matter for once. The HR person says that he will issue a note to everyone to give her some peace. Before the day is out, she has received three emails from co-workers expressing their distress about her distress. They talk about how they can completely understand where she is coming from, but that they were just trying to help, and now of course they are upset as well. She doesn't reply directly to any of them. She just forwards them to HR. After work she receives a text message from Clara on her personal mobile phone – how did she get the number? – promising not to contact her again. But then at her desk in the morning there are some flowers from Clara and later on there is an email promising again not to contact her and apologizing. Abigail feels suffocated, so back to HR she goes. It's getting worse, she says. The HR person wants to set up a meeting between her and Clara to clear the air. Abigail resists. 'Just telling her to stop should be enough,' she says. 'I don't know why I'm having to go through this.' But the HR person pushes and pushes and presents it like it is the only choice, so a meeting is scheduled for two days' time. In the meantime, she finds that colleagues are actively avoiding her, which is also not what she wanted. In fact, it feels much the same as how things were before. It still brings unwanted attention to her. She doesn't get invited to lunch or for after-work drinks anymore. Nobody includes her in funny email threads. When she arrives for the meeting with HR, Clara is there and is already teary. For forty-five minutes Abigail sits in near silence while Clara cries, apologizes and justifies. Abigail keeps waiting for the HR person to step in and stop this show, but he doesn't. Does he think this is going well? This is the problem with men. He was never going to step in to stop Clara's wailing. He doesn't know how to deal with it. 'I really don't need this,' Abigail says to him as Clara blows her nose. 'I'm under enough stress as it is.' 'Oh no,' wails Clara. And then collapses into floods of tears again. 'Do you want to step outside?' Abigail suggests. 'Do you want to go and compose yourself and then when you're ready you can come back in?' 'Clara is very upset,' says the HR person. 'I understand that she has recently lost someone too.' 'That was over two years ago,' says Abigail. 'That's not what this is about.' The HR person feels as though she is being unfair. 'If I cried,' asks Abigail, 'would you be on my side then?'

Chapter Twenty

A SECOND INTERVIEW WITH ABIGAIL

B ell and Sacker stood at the front door after waving away their driver.

'I think it's time to speak to Abigail again,' said Bell.

'Are we nearing the end?' asked Sacker.

'There are just one or two puzzle pieces remaining.'

Mr O'Brien opened the door for them, and Bell asked him to bring Abigail to the library.

'Have you found my brother's killer?' asked Abigail the moment she was through the door. 'Have you finally solved it?'

'I'm afraid I will have to disappoint you a little longer,' said Bell. 'Though I am getting very close to the end, I have not solved this case yet. I just wanted us to meet again in private so that I could go over what I have learned.'

Abigail looked understandably disappointed.

'I thought that this would all be over by now,' she said.

'These things take time,' said Bell. Sacker nodded in agreement. 'We have heard a lot of things here over the past few days. Things that you may not be happy to know,' continued Bell. 'Though much of it has been very illuminating.'

'I'm not sure I understand,' she said cautiously.

'Well, I will fill you in on what I have learned,' he said.

'First, were you aware that your brother had been covering Declan's gambling debts?'

'I mean – that seems very dramatic,' said Abigail. 'I know that Declan likes a flutter every now and then and I think Benjamin said something about helping him out. But it would have been just for a small amount here and there. Declan can be a little silly, I know, but—'

Bell was shaking his head sadly. 'I am very sorry, mademoiselle. But I did tell you from the start that certain things might come out in the course of my investigations which might make you uncomfortable. This is one of them. I think if you were to hire a forensic accountant, you would find that thousands of pounds have been given to Declan over the years to shore up his debts.'

'Th-thousands?' Abigail spluttered. 'I can't believe that Benjamin would have done something like that without consulting me.'

'People can be a little silly when it comes to old friends,' said Sacker. 'He was probably trying to protect you.'

'Indeed, I think that Benjamin has been keeping many things from you – including the fact that the estate is in financial difficulty,' said Bell.

Abigail looked completely startled.

'Yes, I know this will come as a shock to you, but I think that once you contact your brother's solicitor you will find that there is not as much money as you might think.'

Her face was blank.

'We have also heard a number of things about Barbara.'

'Barbara?' said Abigail, flustered. 'But she's just a secretary.'

'Well,' said Bell, 'this is something we have been trying to tease out – whether she was in fact just a secretary.'

Abigail seemed puzzled.

'What do you mean?'

'Come, come, mademoiselle. You did not think it strange that your brother invited his employee to stay with you over the holiday? Because other people in the house very definitely did. Did you ever notice anything between them?'

'No, no.' Abigail's voice was appalled. 'Absolutely not.'

Bell paused. 'Ah! I knew there was something I needed to ask. Did you do the post the day before yesterday?'

Abigail fixed him with a gaze that was a mix of confusion and anger.

'No.'

'Did anyone else in the house go to the post office? Perhaps Mr O'Brien?'

'No.'

'Is your brother left- or right-handed?

'Left-handed.'

'Ah,' said Bell. He raised a single finger. 'And also, I noted your collective surprise when Cormac mentioned that he and Olivia were engaged – do you know her well? Do you have any reticence about their engagement?'

'Oh, no. Not at all,' Abigail said, her words tumbling out. 'I think I was just shocked because of everything that was going on. I mean, I've only met Olivia once or twice.'

'Do you know anything about her background?' asked Bell playfully.

'No,' said Abigail. 'I can't say I do. Benjamin probably did . . .'

*

Only a couple of months before, Abigail had been apprehensive about her upcoming birthday. The big three-oh had felt somewhat ominous. Now she is ashamed of how shallow she'd been. Two weeks previously, Frances had texted her about celebrating the day and Abigail had said no. She had tried to convince her that 'it would be good for you to see everyone' and Abigail had resisted. She had suggested a weekend away or going for a fancy dinner and Abigail had still said no. Then, a week ago, Abigail had received another text, Frances now looking to have 'just a small get together with the girls', and Abigail had relented. She insisted, however, that there would be no presents, a small pre-approved guest list and that it would happen during the day at her own house. Just a simple pot-luck lunch. Something calm. Low key. Frances said she was on it. 'It'll do you good,' she said. And so, on the day, the small group of five women arrive at Abigail's house with cake and bowls of potato salad and small talk. Some people share news: job promotions, a new baby niece, a house purchase, a holiday booked. Frances has brought a bottle of champagne and insists that everyone has 'just a sip'. The smell of the champagne makes Abigail feel sick and she has to put her glass down. She excuses herself and goes upstairs to sit on her bed. She doesn't want to throw up or faint in front of everyone. The last time she had champagne was . . . She takes a series of calming breaths and then spends a couple of minutes tidying clothes away in her wardrobe until she has reached equilibrium again. By the time Abigail has come back downstairs, Frances has put on some music and has started dancing. She is shaking her champagne glass in the air. Others are joining in. They are smiling and laughing and moving to the music. Frances grabs Abigail's hand and pulls her to them. Abigail tries to pull back, but Frances has a surprisingly strong grip. She can't get away. 'Stop it,' she says. She digs her nails into Frances's wrist. Frances cries out and swears. 'What did you do that for?' The others have stopped dancing. Someone is fumbling with the music, trying to turn it off. 'Jesus, what's wrong with you?' This has been a mistake and Abigail needs it all to stop. 'Get out,' she says. 'Get out, get out, everyone get out.' Everyone starts to leave except Frances. The others share little looks as they put down their glasses and head for the front door. They talk in whispers outside while getting into their cars. The WhatsApp group will be full of speculation. Abigail wants to physically assault them all. She wants to cause them bodily harm. Frances is still there. 'What's gotten into you?' she asks. 'I told you I wanted something quiet,' Abigail says. 'In fact, I told you I didn't want this at all. My brother's dead. How can you be dancing in my front room when my brother's dead?' Her friend is silent for a moment. 'I thought you would enjoy this. I thought it would be good to get your mind off things. You seemed fine,' says Frances. And those final words hit her in the chest like a train.

'I seemed fine?' Abigail repeats. 'I mean . . .' says Frances, 'you're handling things remarkably well. I'm in awe of you. If I was in your situation, I wouldn't be able to get out of bed. I'd be crying constantly.' Abigail sways a little. 'It took me three hours to get out of bed this morning,' she says. 'And I cry all the time. I'm barely able to get through the day.' Frances's face is blank. 'Well, I didn't know. I mean, you never said. I can't read your mind.' Abigail thinks she will faint. 'Can't read my mind?' She is incredulous. 'No one is asking you to read my mind. Do you have any sense at all? My brother is dead. It's been less than two months now and because I seem presentable and I can walk upright you think I'm fine. How could I possibly be fine? How will I ever be fine again?' But Frances has become defensive. 'How am I supposed to know how you're dealing with it? You never tell me anything.' Abigail has a million things she could say but she raises her hand and just slaps her instead.

Chapter Twenty-One

THE POLICE MAKE AN ARREST

'And how long has Olivia—'

But they were interrupted by the butler.

'Mr Bell, there is a phone call for you,' he said, and he led Bell to the office before closing the door behind him.

'This is Bell.'

On the other end of the line, he heard the growling voice of Detective Inspector Ferret.

'Bell, I have some news for you. We have arrested a member of the smuggling ring. We have him in custody now.'

'Congratulations, Inspector! Do you have any idea if he is connected to my murder?'

'Not yet. We'll look into everything, of course, but this gang are pretty sophisticated. This murder doesn't seem like their type of work.'

Ferret rang off and Bell returned to the drawing room, where Sacker and Abigail were waiting expectantly.

'That was Detective Inspector Ferret. He tells me that they have arrested two members of the jewellery-smuggling ring.'

'What does that mean for us?' asked Abigail.

'I am not sure, mademoiselle. But the inspector is sending

some men to do a search of the grounds. Hopefully the police will have more information soon.'

'What does this mean?' asked Abigail. 'Are we getting closer to the truth?'

'Yes, I believe so.'

*

After her father's death, Abigail had availed herself of ten free counselling sessions provided to her by her university. She didn't make it to all ten: the first counsellor went AWOL after the initial session and when she eventually contacted the college, they hurriedly sent her to someone else. The second counsellor wanted to analyze her dreams and though Abigail wanted to run, it felt churlish to get through two counsellors in less than a month. Especially when the service was free. During their sessions, she barely talked. She didn't know how to start. How many different ways can you say you're sad your mom and dad are dead? How many times can you say that you rarely remember your dreams? She went for six sessions before feigning glandular fever. Benjamin didn't go to any therapy – not that she knew of – though now that she thinks about it, she never told him that she herself was going. And here she was, back again, unsure whether it was really for her. The therapist was nice enough. Young and calm with searching eyes. But Abigail wished there was more of a back and forth, more of a conversation between them. Maybe a bit of tension. A bit of an argument. She didn't enjoy the constant prompting of 'and why do you think that is?' She was not lacking in self-awareness. She could parse her own thoughts. In fact, all she did was think about and agonize over her feelings. Now, she is here to talk about Benjamin, of course, but the therapist keeps asking about her childhood and her parents' deaths. She needs to talk about Benjamin. She needs to get her thoughts in order. 'Did you feel a similar way after your parents died?' asks the therapist. An image of her mother suddenly comes to her – a cannula in her arm, that smell of a hospital. 'I didn't. Those were different deaths. I was sad, of course – terribly, horrifyingly, heartbreakingly sad – and still am, but my mother had been unwell. We knew she was going to die; it didn't come as a shock. And my father was in an accident but it . . . with Benjamin I don't know what happened . . .' The therapist nods. 'I just think that we need to look at the big picture,' she says. 'You've had a lot of trauma in your life.' Abigail bristles at the word and the therapist notices. 'You don't think of these as traumas?' 'I think . . .' She pauses for a moment. 'I just don't like the word. I don't want to be a victim.' The therapist nods. 'That's understandable. Very few people want to be thought of in that way. And you don't have to be a victim. This isn't about that. This is about a trauma – yes, I'm using that word again – happening to you and you deciding that you need some assistance in coping with that.' Abigail thinks for a little while. 'What I want,' she says, 'is to figure out what Benjamin . . . why he died . . . and what . . .' 'You don't have a narrative around it,' the therapist suggests. 'I know the sequence of events,' Abigail says. 'Is that enough for you?' Another prompting question. 'No. That's why I'm here.' The therapist shifts in her seat. 'We need stories to organize experiences and process our emotions. Your search for a story is a way to understand your brother's death. Wanting answers is totally understandable, Abigail. This is part of the grieving process for you. This is you making sense of what happened. But I think it's important that you don't become overly focused on a conclusion.' 'But if there isn't a conclusion,' Abigail asks, 'how will I ever move on?' 'That's why you're here,' the therapist says. 'It is very unlikely that you will get to the truth of what happened, but I think it could be possible for you to arrive at *a* truth. By that, I mean I think it could be possible for you to come to an understanding of what happened – an eagle's eye view of the situation – without knowing every single piece of minutiae. I'm going to help you get to that point. Do you want to work with me on this?' Abigail nods. 'Good, okay. Now, tell me about your parents.'

Chapter Twenty-Two

BELL CONDUCTS AN EXPERIMENT

Bell was deep in conversation with Detective Inspector Ferret, all of his attention pressed on the small slip of paper Ferret had handed him a moment before. The detective inspector was talking animatedly, and Bell's head was down in a pensive manner. Once the inspector had finished talking, Bell thanked him, closed the door behind him, and returned to the library where Sacker was waiting.

'What were you discussing with the inspector?' asked Sacker.

'We were discussing the past,' said Bell, contemplatively.

'The past?' said Sacker, surprised. 'Have his men arrived yet?'

'Yes,' said Bell. 'He has them searching the grounds.'

'Well, in the meantime, I'm not sure how pertinent this is—' Sacker said.

'Tell me anyway, Sacker. You're not good at separating good information from bad.'

'Well, I went into the drawing room to fetch my hat and I came upon Margaret and Declan. I startled them a little, I have to say. They were standing very close together – quite intimately – and I was wondering if maybe there was something going on between them.'

'Did you hear anything they said? Please tell me exactly.'

'Declan was talking about money. Something about money being a solution to a problem.'

'And what was your impression of Margaret? Was she angry or annoyed?'

'She seemed, honestly, a little bit scared.'

'Hmmm, that is interesting. Thank you, Sacker. This has been very helpful.' Bell checked his watch. 'Oh yes, I'm just in time for my little experiment. I need you to gather Stephen and Cormac and I will meet you all outside under the balcony.'

Sacker went off without another word. While he was waiting, Bell went around the back of the house to inspect the shed. His eyes glanced over the various tools, gardening implements and bottles of pesticides.

'Bell? Bell? Where are you?' Sacker was calling him. Bell emerged from the shed into the winter sunlight.

'Ah, thank you very much, Sacker. Now, Stephen and Cormac, I need a little help. I have an experiment. Do you see this balcony here?' Bell pointed up to the first floor. 'I need you both to try to get to that balcony from the outside. You may use any method you wish but quick and easy is the key.'

Cormac went first. He got hold of the trellis and made his way a couple of feet off the ground before a piece of the wood came off in his hand and he nearly fell. He looked for another route where the wooden trellis wasn't rotten, but Bell already had his answer. Stephen had located a small stepladder in the shed. He climbed it slowly but when he reached the top he was still too far from the balcony. He stretched to see if he could pull himself up.

'Even if you were a foot taller,' said Sacker, 'you would still need to have incredible upper body strength to get onto the balcony.'

The two men had to admit defeat. One of the young policemen who was helping to search the grounds asked to have a go and Bell was happy to let him. The policeman opted for a slightly different route up the trellis – more directly under the balcony – with the idea that he could pull himself up and over the railings. He was a strong, agile young man and managed to climb the trellis ably, but he too found it impossible to reach his destination. Failure again.

However, on his way down the policeman spotted something. Stuck in the wooden trellis was a small piece of ripped brown cloth. He carefully removed it and presented it to Bell.

'Do you think this might be a clue?' the policeman enquired.

Bell put on his glasses and inspected it. 'Ah, yes, thank you,' he said eventually.

'Did you find something?' asked Sacker.

'This is a very remarkable piece of cloth. Most remarkable,' said Bell.

'What do you mean?' asked Sacker.

'I mean that it is remarkable the police did not see it before now. Nearly as though it hadn't been there earlier,' said Bell.

Suddenly there was consternation from around the side of the house and Barbara came running to them.

'Come quickly,' she exclaimed. 'The police have found someone lurking on the grounds.'

'Good god,' said Bell, and they all hurried towards the source of the noise.

Two police officers had a hold of a bearded man. The man was yelling and pleading with them to let him go.

'Please, please, there's been a mistake,' the man said.

'Just steady on there now,' said a policeman.

'What is going on?' asked Bell.

'While we were conducting our search of the grounds, sir, we found this man prowling with a bag of weapons.'

'I wasn't prowling. I wasn't – I have permission to be here,' the man said. 'And I don't have any weapons.'

'He tried to run when we spotted him, but we managed to grab him and bring him here.'

Bell got close to the man so that he could properly see his face. He was a man aged beyond his years. Deep grooves marked his weathered skin. He looked completely defeated.

'This is a mistake,' he was saying. 'I haven't done anything wrong.'

'He has weapons,' said the other policeman, indicating a canvas bag which had been tossed to the ground. Bell picked it up and inspected its contents: there was a screwdriver, a hammer, and a saw.

'I was only returning them,' the man said.

'You mean you stole them,' said Sacker.

'No, I borrowed them. I'm the gardener here. I know I'm not supposed to take tools off the premises, but I can't feed my family on a part-time job. I got some work at a farm nearby and so I needed the tools for that. I am so sorry, but I didn't mean any harm. I was trying to return them.'

'Get Abigail,' Bell said to Sacker. 'She'll clear up this mess.'

Sacker ran inside and quickly returned with Abigail.

'Francis, what are you doing here?' she asked immediately.

'I'm so sorry,' the man was still saying. 'I didn't mean any harm.'

'Mademoiselle, you recognize this man?'

'Yes, he's the gardener.'

'Ah, so he was telling the truth,' said Bell. 'Please let the man go.'

But the policemen held on to him all the same.

'I told you. I told you. I was just returning these tools.' He turned to Abigail. 'I am so sorry, miss. I heard about your brother. I wanted to return them without disturbing you but now I've caused all this fuss.'

'It is no trouble,' said Abigail. 'I don't mind you borrowing tools. It's nothing to me.'

'We'd like to take him in for questioning,' said a policeman.

'Is that really necessary?'

'We have to do our due diligence, ma'am.'

Francis's head was down. A single tear fell onto the loose gravel.

'Well, please do not put him in handcuffs,' said Abigail. 'I will phone later to make sure that he's been released. This man has worked for my family for years. He is no threat to me. They just have some questions for you, Francis. Please answer them honestly.'

CHALLENGE TO THE READER

As is his custom, Auguste Bell would now like to invite you, the reader, to ruminate on the central question of this book: who is the murderer?

At this point in the narrative, you should have everything you need to solve the crime.

You should, through use of logic and deduction, be able to not merely guess, but prove, the identity of the culprit. You should also be able to explain how the murder occurred, and indeed, why.

Good luck.

*

Stephen opens his front door as Abigail is getting out of the car and comes out to greet her. He hugs her tightly and kisses the top of her head before putting his arm around her shoulders and pulling her inside with a small 'c'mon.' They sit at his kitchen table, facing each other. Stephen is leaning in and holding her hands. 'I have nothing for you to eat,' he says. Abigail doesn't mind; she's not hungry. 'Oh, but I was just at the shop, and I should have . . . I could make you some tea . . . ?' She shakes her head. 'I've drunk so much tea . . .' 'Of course.' Stephen laughs softly. They are sitting so close together that their knees are touching. 'I need to ask you some things,' Abigail whispers. 'Yeah, yeah okay.' Stephen whispers too. She looks into his eyes. 'Did you suspect something?' she asks. Stephen fully clasps her hands in his. 'I've been going over this in my head,' he says. 'And obviously with the Guards – I spoke to them and . . . there is nothing. It makes no sense to me. I didn't see anything, and I don't know how I didn't.' He is staring at her, and it is so intense that she has to look away. 'I failed him. And I failed you. I must have missed something. I just don't know what.' Abigail is looking down at the table. 'I didn't see anything either,' she says. 'It isn't your fault.' 'No, no, don't do that. It's not your . . . no, no.' The clock ticks. The fridge gurgles. A car drives past outside. 'I keep going over it. Was there something else that night? He had a couple of drinks . . . I mean we had all been drinking . . . did they do a toxicology report?' 'There was nothing . . .' she says. 'I must have missed something. I mean, my best friend died. My best friend is dead. He doesn't exist anymore.' Stephen shakes his head. A muscle in Abigail's back is tingling. She is getting a familiar feeling. 'I've been reading, hold on . . .' says Stephen. He goes to another room before returning to the kitchen with a small book. 'Someone gave me this. I'm not a poetry fan but I've been dipping in and out of it over these last months and there was one here . . . some lines stood out to me . . .' He starts reading from a poem. Abigail doesn't really understand it, but she can see how affected Stephen is. He skips forward a few pages and then reads another couple of lines. Abigail just nods like a polite audience member. 'That's what I read at the funeral,' he said. 'And it's really stayed with me for some reason. There's just something about that poem that feels like Benjamin. Something about his grace and kindness. Does that make sense?' Abigail nods softly. She wants to reach out and touch his arm. Stephen is turning the pages of the book. 'I need to tell you something as well. I've accepted a job offer. In Warsaw.' 'In Warsaw?' 'Ana's family live not far from there, and my company has offices . . . I need something new. A break. I need to start afresh. And Ana doesn't like being so far away from home.' 'But you're leaving?' 'Yes, these last few months have really made me evaluate things. I need to get out of Ireland for a while. It's a drag. To be honest, Abigail, you should get out of here too. You need a fresh start. Go somewhere else and live a life. This country is so small.' She nods. 'I'm being serious. You don't have to stay here. You don't have to do any of this anymore. Go abroad. Live your life. Your job has offices all over Europe. You should put in for a transfer.' Abigail breathes out slowly. She sees flashes of how he was as a teenager. She wants to rage against him, shove him, beat his chest. Call him selfish. Tell him he is only thinking of himself. 'Are you angry at me?' he asks. 'No, I'm not angry at you.' But her voice is hard. 'You sound angry, and I mean . . . look, this is just something I have to do. I have to find a way to move on with my life. Christ, my best friend died and . . .' 'My brother died.' 'It isn't a competition,' says Stephen. There is an edge to his voice. How suddenly it can appear, she thinks. 'I need to do what's best for me.' 'You always do,' Abigail says mainly to herself. She has stood up. 'Excuse me?' 'You always do,' she repeats and Stephen blinks. 'You're grieving right now, and I understand that. But it is still not okay for you to make me feel bad about this decision. Are you expecting me to just stay here for ever like your keeper?' 'I'm not expecting you to do anything. It just . . . triggered a memory in me, that's all. I've only just remembered. You've always been like this.' 'Like what?' 'Self-ish.' Stephen is genuinely taken aback. She may as well say it all now. 'Everything's about you. Every conversation is about you. Even now, you keep talking about Benjamin as *your* best friend. He's not your anything. He's *my* brother.' 'I need to be able to talk about my feelings . . .' 'Yes, but not to me. Talk to your girlfriend, a friend, talk to your therapist. Have some cop-on. Do you think I need this? Do you think I need the burden of your feelings right now? You're supposed to be supporting me, not the other way around.' Stephen's features have hardened. 'We're all grieving,' he says. 'You don't have a monopoly on that. What am I supposed to do? Just give up? Just stop living? I don't want to be stuck being sad all the time. Whether you like it or not, life goes on. We can't wake him for ever.' Abigail just stares at him. 'You kissed me,' she says. It is practically a whimper. 'What?' asks Stephen. He looks genuinely confused. 'You kissed me,' she says, fractionally louder. 'What?' he repeats. 'I didn't . . . I haven't kissed you.' 'You kissed me,' she says, now more forcefully. 'That night. After everyone had gone to bed. We were outside. By the firepit. Clearing up. And you kissed me.' 'Oh,' he says, and he shakes his head at the memory. 'I was drinking. It was a party. I have no idea why you're bringing this up now . . . everything that has happened since. I mean, I have a girlfriend.' 'I know you have a girlfriend,' she says. Her voice is at a normal level now. 'You had a girlfriend that night too.' Stephen breathes out as though he is talking to a child. 'Oh, c'mon Abigail. It was – what? – a drunken kiss. This is silly teenage bullshit.' Her eyes are filling with tears now. She wants to tell him that she knows it's silly teenage bullshit. She knows she's being immature. She knows it didn't mean anything. Even at the time she knew it was just some fleeting moment, that it wasn't the start of a great love story. She knows he has a girlfriend. She knows this will never go anywhere. She doesn't want it to anyway. She knows, she knows, she knows. But she also knows that he is getting away with something. He is not an idiot. He knew what he was doing. Something has happened to her that means that she needs to be comforted right now in this moment. She needs some hope, some solace. She needs him to be kind to her. She needs him to lie to her. He is being so cruel, and it is unnecessary. And anything she says will just make it worse. So, she decides to not say anything. She blinks and the tears fall from her eyes. Stephen looks away. And she can't bear it. She gets up. He starts to say something, but she is already out of the kitchen, through the hallway and grasping at the handle of her car door. She wonders if he might come after her. But of course, he doesn't.

Chapter Twenty-Three

A SOLUTION

'Of course!' Bell declared suddenly. 'How could I have been such a fool!'

He called out to Sacker.

'Please, Sacker, gather everyone in the drawing room.'

'Have you found a solution?'

'Yes, I have. Just now. And I have been so stupid. I can't believe it. It was right in front of my eyes. Now, please do hurry. We can't waste any more time.'

Sacker went off to gather everyone. The household swiftly made their way to the drawing room as Bell had requested. They were all dressed formally for dinner. Bell was there waiting, standing imperiously in front of them. The room bubbled silently with anticipation.

Once the door had closed heavily behind the last of them, Bell began.

'At first, I believed this to be a very tricky case. A locked-door mystery always is, naturally. My mind has been a little scrambled with all the confusion and misdirection and smokescreens and red herrings. But when I finally managed to clear my head, I realized that I had been wrong. This was not a tricky case after all, in fact it was a very simple one.

The basic facts of the case are that a man is found dead in a locked house with a closed circle of suspects. Therefore, the murderer has to be somebody here in this room. I will admit to being stumped for a long time. It felt as though I had been given too many clues – many of them contradictory. But once I homed in on the basics of the case, everything started to become clear. I have found in my past experiences that most motives are derived from the basest elements of human life: money,' Bell said, looking at Declan, 'or love,' he turned towards Margaret, 'jealousy,' he intoned, looking at Stephen, 'or obscuration,' he said, finally looking towards Olivia and Cormac. 'But none of these quite fit with the clues at hand.'

'Have you found the murderer?' asked Abigail. She was tugging impatiently at the sleeves of her dress.

'Yes, Abigail,' said Bell. 'I have. It is so simple and in fact, I knew it from the start. I realize now why I was so confused: this was, on one hand, a crime of passion, of great emotion, of retribution and of pure hatred. And yet on the other hand this is a crime that was committed so very carefully and method-ically. I started to think about whose personality fit this description. This was not a crime committed for gain – this was a crime committed in vengeance. A crime committed out of great resentment and anger. A resentment that had been concealed for many years. This person had the opportunity to kill, and they took it.

'Let us go over the facts of that morning. Most of the party had already convened downstairs when you realized that Benjamin had not joined you. Initially, you thought nothing of this. It had been a long night and Benjamin was probably still sleeping it off. And so, Stephen was dispatched to wake him. He returned downstairs a couple of minutes later, appearing a little worried. He said that he had tried the door but to his great surprise it was locked. He had knocked gently but gotten no answer. He had knocked again, more forcefully, but still nothing. He had called out Benjamin's name but there was no response. This would seem out of character – the locked door, the late sleeping, the lack of a response. You were all a little worried now. As a group, you proceeded upstairs to check again. Stephen tried the door once more in vain and now you – Margaret – began to knock very forcefully. And so, the next logical thing to do was, of course, break down the door – which Declan did. You all tumbled into the room to find Benjamin dead.'

Bell paused here for effect.

'This is the sequence of events that everybody has laid out for me. Exactly that. But the human mind is an interesting thing, and it can be so easily manipulated. Let me see . . . Margaret, did you attempt to open the door that morning?'

Margaret looked a little taken aback.

'Well, of course. You've just said. We tried the door, and it was locked.'

'*We* tried the door,' Bell repeated. 'But did *you*?'

Margaret was confused.

'I don't know—'

'In the simplest of terms, mademoiselle, did you turn the handle?'

Margaret's eyes were frantic.

'Er, no, I don't think so. I just knocked. But I can't see—'

'If you did not try the handle of the door,' interrupted Bell, 'how do you know that the door was locked?'

Margaret's face suddenly cleared.

'Because Stephen told me it was locked,' she said.

'Ah, yes, because Stephen told you it was locked,' said Bell. 'And you did not question him, because of course he put on a great show of trying the handle and knocking and shouting. A very good show.'

The group en masse had turned towards Stephen, who was sitting very still.

'I believe this is what happened: in the night, after everyone had gone to bed, Stephen made his way to Benjamin's room. Perhaps he was looking to talk or argue – I am unsure about his exact mood at this point. He opened the door – yes, opened, the door was of course unlocked – and there he found a slumbering Benjamin. Asleep but still very much alive.

'And then something broke in him. He saw his old friend there asleep and vulnerable, and he made a fatal decision. For, you see, Stephen deeply resented his old friend. A resentment that he kept very well hidden over the years. But it was a resentment that had grown into a deep hatred. Benjamin was the star pupil, the fine rugby player, a man who was never without a female companion, a man of wealth and luxury. Everything in Benjamin's life seemed easy and Stephen resented that.' Bell was standing in front of Stephen now. 'You are unhappy with your life. You hid your feelings well, sir, but you allowed flashes to show over the years. You had a clear motive. And now, of course, you had an opportunity. You strangled Benjamin with a ligature, and then quietly returned to your own room. The next morning you thought of this ruse of the locked door to confuse and confound.'

'Stephen, oh my god! Is this true?' Abigail's eyes were filled with tears.

'Of course not,' Stephen replied in a low growl. 'The whole thing is pure conjecture. No evidence. Absolutely ridiculous.'

'I am very sorry, Abigail. I am well aware of your feelings for Stephen and how this means that you have now lost both of the important men in your life,' said Bell.

'You were always my number-one suspect, Steve,' said Declan.

'It doesn't seem like a lot of hard evidence,' said Margaret. 'I can't see it standing up in a court of law.'

'Doesn't it make a lot more sense, though, that one of those burglars got in?' said Abigail, panic in her face. 'The unlocked balcony door, the piece of fabric. I mean, Stephen has known Benjamin his whole life—'

'Ah, the piece of fabric in the trellis! Stephen needed to distract attention away from himself and the rest of the house, and so when he heard about the existence of the jewellery-smuggling ring in Chapter Fourteen, he decided to implicate them in the murder. He took one of his jackets and ripped it, placing the piece of fabric somewhere we would find it. That was what was missing from your wardrobe when I went looking through your room. He took advantage of the fact that you, Barbara, had been woken in the night by someone trying to open your bedroom door and the fact that Abigail and Cormac had heard something outside that night too. Indeed, I think he may have encouraged these uncovered memories. He just needed to place this evidence on the trellis outside to give the impression that that is how the killer gained entry to the room, and to tie it back to the ring who he assumed would never be caught and therefore neither would he.'

'It all sounds so incredible,' said Cormac.

'And yet . . .'

Stephen was looking at Abigail, who was crying gently.

'Abigail, please. This is nonsense. This man doesn't know what he is talking about. I loved Benjamin. I would never do anything like this. You know that. Please. All of this is just some story. There is no proof.'

'Ah, that is where you are wrong,' said Bell simply. 'You can bring him in now, Sacker.'

Sacker opened the drawing room door and in stepped Detective Inspector Ferret. He was holding a crumpled brown jacket.

'Good evening,' the Detective Inspector said solemnly.

'Is this your jacket, Stephen?'

'I – I don't . . .'

Ferret held the jacket aloft and moved it to reveal the missing piece of fabric. Declan stood up and inspected it.

'It has your monogram, Steve,' he said.

'Oh god,' exclaimed Margaret, and she rushed to Abigail's side. Stephen was still trying to talk to her.

'Abigail, please. Abigail, I can— This isn't evidence of anything—'

'Step away from her, sir,' said Bell.

Declan placed himself in between Stephen and Abigail.

'Take a seat, Steve.'

'Actually, I don't think there'll be a need for that,' said the detective inspector. 'We're taking you in.'

Stephen was handcuffed, and as he was led away, he cried out, 'Abigail, Abigail, please—'

*

'I didn't see that ending coming,' said Sacker.

'Yes, me neither,' said Bell. He was looking down at his shoes. His mind still elsewhere.

'You don't seem very pleased with your solution. Give yourself a break. You got him, Bell!'

'Did I?'

＊

Abigail nearly starts to cry just seeing the pile of post on the floor of the hallway. She gathers up all the envelopes and glances through them: there are bills and junk mail and several issues of a magazine. All things she will need to cancel or pay. The apartment is frozen in time. It still has remnants of Christmas – cards displayed on the bookshelf and a small tree. There are dishes piled up on the drying tray, a shampoo bottle lying on its side in the shower, half-read books next to the bed. Margaret is the only person Abigail would have asked to help with something like this and in the end, she didn't have to ask at all – Margaret brought it up first. Abigail had spent months diligently ignoring the issue of the flat, pushing it further and further down her to-do list until Margaret contacted her one day out of the blue suggesting that she would deal with it herself. But Abigail didn't want her to clear it completely on her own – there were too many potential clues to find – so instead she compromised, and they set a date for both of them to do it together. Margaret will be here soon, but Abigail has something to do first. She is looking for a diary. First, she checks Benjamin's room – the bed unmade, the pillow still holding the shape of his head. She rifles through

the drawers in his bedside locker and then searches the ward-
robe. It smells of him, she feels the arms of his shirts against
her cheek and wonders what she is going to do with all of
them. There are some shoe boxes filled with old tickets and
programmes, but no diary. A whole box full of their parents'
wedding photographs. She sits on the floor and fans them out
in front of her: her aunt in a blue taffeta dress, a sleeping
flower girl, a table full of pints. Everyone is so beautiful and
young. In the little office he had created in his spare room,
she checks through his desk drawers, finding plenty of things
that should be returned to his employer, but no diary. He
didn't seem like the diary type, she has to admit. She never
even remembered him having one growing up. His work
laptop is still there. She opens it and switches it on but
doesn't know the password. There is a knock at the front door.
Margaret is very business-like. She has brought bin bags and
cardboard boxes with her. As they walk through the apartment
together, Margaret makes the odd comment like 'Ah, books in
here as well' and 'I know someone who is looking for an arm-
chair'. They form a plan of action. Margaret feels like they
could get a large amount done today. 'I have some time off
coming up so I can come over whenever to finish up,' she says.
Margaret has a tendency to take over and Abigail finds it easy
to fall into her slipstream. Margaret wants to start with linens
and towels and clothes. Abigail retreats to the safety of the
kitchen, with its lack of intimacy. She starts removing bowls
and plates and coffee cups from cupboards and placing them
in boxes. She doesn't recognize any of them. And they seem
very much not Benjamin's style. She wonders where they will
go, who will take them. There is a blender and countless

kitchen utensils and pots and pans. A used glass in the sink with his fingerprints on it. And it suddenly all seems so overwhelming. There are so many things – suddenly useless, just taking up space. She thinks about all the objects she has in her house and how she doesn't need most of them, and she feels a little dizzy and has to sit down at the kitchen table. The kitchen table – that was another thing that needed to go. Hopefully the new owners of the flat would be willing to take it. Maybe they would take the sofa and coffee table and bed frame too. She would give them everything and anything they wanted. The estate agent had been very optimistic. She said that it was a seller's market. They would find a buyer no problem. And it would be good to get the property marketed before the summer rush. Benjamin had only been living here for four years. His first purchase after renting for a long while. Abigail is sure he had plans for this place and for the next one after that. But she feels no real attachment. This isn't home to her. Abigail decides to join Margaret in the bedroom. She's just going to ask. There is nothing to lose. She will show her hand, though her hand is worth nothing if she doesn't get an answer. 'Did Benjamin . . .' Abigail starts. She clears her throat. 'Did Benjamin ever keep a diary when you were together? You know, a journal or something . . .' Margaret pauses for a moment. 'No, not that I know of. I don't really think of Benjamin as the journal type. Why do you ask?' 'Oh, well. I suppose . . .' Margaret stops putting bed linen into black plastic bags. 'Oh, I see,' she says. 'Yes, it would be handy, but I don't think . . . we can look, of course.' Abigail doesn't bother telling her that she already has. 'I'm going to bring these all home and wash them and then I'll send them to that charity

I was telling you about,' Margaret says, starting to load things in the bags again. 'We can do the same with his clothes. You can go through them. And, erm . . .' She stops. She isn't looking at Abigail. She has a large bedsheet in her hand that she is absentmindedly folding. 'I might like to keep something, if that's okay. Just a shirt or . . . I don't know. I hope it's okay. I won't . . . It's up to you.' 'Of course,' Abigail says. 'Take whatever you want.' 'He has a jacket I like. He wore it a lot one summer. It really suited him,' says Margaret. 'You should take that,' Abigail says. 'The charity is very good,' continues Margaret. 'A friend of mine volunteers for them. That's how I heard about them.' Something occurs to Abigail. A feeling that she had forgotten about. 'Were you back together at the time of his death?' Abigail asks. Margaret looks up at her, surprised. 'Why do you . . . ? No,' she says. 'No, we weren't.' 'Oh,' says Abigail. 'I thought when you came to the house together. I thought I saw something between you. A closeness or something.' 'Nothing,' says Margaret. She is looking at Abigail intently. 'I did love your brother, though.' 'Oh, it's not that,' says Abigail. 'I just really thought there was some reignited spark between you.' 'That was all a long time ago,' says Margaret, and Abigail nods. 'Can you tell me – that day when you drove down, before you got to the house . . . how was he?' Margaret thinks for a moment. She wants to be exact. 'He was the same as he always was.' 'That's what everyone has been saying. I don't understand how none of us spotted anything.' 'I don't understand it either. I would have noticed if something had been off. You can't live with someone and hide things like that for ever.' 'So, what happened?' But Margaret can't answer that. 'You were late arriving at the house,' says

Abigail. 'What did you do?' They collected – Benjamin and Declan – collected me from my house and we headed down. We stopped to get some petrol and . . . nothing really . . . we played some music, and we were talking about inconsequential stuff, I can't even remember now – Christmas, work, plans for the New Year, that kind of thing. And then, well, Benjamin suddenly decided he wanted to stop somewhere first. A small beach. He seemed to remember it when we were on the road. There were no signposts, but he directed Declan there. Right here, left there, down tiny, unmarked roads. And I was complaining to him. We were going to be late, and I didn't want to be on some freezing cold beach in December. And we arrived at this cove which was completely empty, and we got out of the car, and we were maybe there for twenty minutes. We just sat there for a while and skimmed stones. And it was so cold, so bracing. I got back into the car and Declan put on the heat, but Benjamin stayed on the beach a little longer. I admit that I was annoyed at the time but now I view it differently. I was glad, after . . .' But Margaret can't go on. She is sobbing and Abigail is holding her. There is something about seeing Margaret break down like this that makes her feel stronger somehow. Margaret never cries, never allows emotion to overcome her. She is always the stoic one. 'I can't believe he's gone,' Margaret says. 'It is so unfair. He deserved more than this.' 'Deserve is a strange word,' says Abigail. 'It's the correct one,' says Margaret. 'I imagined he would be in my life for ever.' 'Me too,' says Abigail. 'But now I'll just be in your life for ever. If you'll have me,' says Margaret, wiping her tears away. Abigail laughs. 'Is this a proposal?' she asks. 'It's a threat.' They both laugh then. Margaret is drying her eyes. 'Well, this place won't pack up itself.' She is suddenly herself again. 'Stephen is going to Warsaw,' says Abigail. 'He's moving there for work and for his girlfriend.' 'Yes, that sounds like Stephen,' says Margaret. 'It's unfortunate that you can't depend on him. I know you had a little crush on him. And there's nothing wrong with Stephen, obviously, but he looks out for himself a little bit too much, you know?' And Abigail did know. 'He let Benjamin down a couple of times. And they had some rows but . . . well, that doesn't matter anymore. So many things don't matter anymore,' Margaret says.

Chapter Twenty-Four

ANOTHER SOLUTION

'Of course!' Bell declared suddenly. 'How could I have been such a fool!'

He called out to Sacker.

'Please, Sacker, gather everyone in the drawing room.'

'Have you found a solution?'

'Yes, I have. Just now. And I have been so stupid. I can't believe it. It was right in front of my eyes. Now, please do hurry. We can't waste any more time.'

Sacker went off to gather everyone. The household promptly made their way to the drawing room as Bell had requested. They were all dressed formally for dinner. Bell was there waiting, standing imperiously in front of them. The room bubbled silently with anticipation.

Once the door had closed heavily behind the last of them, Bell began.

'The key to any murder enquiry is motive. Motive is the key that unlocks the door to the solution. And while the world is a diverse place and people are complex beings, murder is not complicated. In fact, motives for most murders, in my opinion, are for trivial matters. It could be love or revenge or jealousy. The very basest of human emotions. And once I turned my attention towards possible motives for this crime, at once it became clear.'

'So, you know who the murderer is?' said Abigail, rising slightly from her seat.

'Yes, mademoiselle, I do,' said Bell simply. The faces of the group paled in front of him. 'I realized right away that this was a crime of passion. A crime of great hate or love – quite often these are the same thing. People can do terrible things for love or the lack of it.'

Bell's eyes moved across the guests in front of him.

'You love your brother don't you, Abigail?'

'Yes, of course,' she replied.

Stephen looked appalled at the question.

'He was a man loved by many,' said Bell. 'Indeed, Declan you loved your friend, didn't you?'

'Yes, my best friend,' said Declan. 'Though admittedly I did not treat him how he deserved.'

'I recall my interview with you in Chapter Twelve where you were very candid about your own faults and the difficulties in your friendship. You were very forthcoming and yet—you purposely left something out, you omitted something very important. It seems that you have not quite recovered enough from your addiction. I could see in your eyes that as we spoke about that night you had a realization about something. Your mind drifted off. Could you be up-front with me now and tell me what this realization was?'

'I don't know what you are—'

'Ah, well. I was hoping for honesty, but I suspect that is too much to ask,' said Bell. 'I will just have to do it myself. A little earlier this afternoon Sacker spotted you in a compromising position with Margaret—'

It was now Margaret's turn to be appalled.

'How dare you! That's an outrageous allegation. You don't know what you saw,' said Margaret. 'We were merely speaking. Absolutely nothing else. How dare you insinuate anything else.'

'You are correct in what you say. "You don't know what you saw". That is true. Sacker did not know but I did. I realized at once what this covert whispering was about. He was attempting to blackmail you, mademoiselle.'

'Nonsense!' declared Declan. Margaret merely spluttered.

'It was blackmail, sir. You still have those gambling debts – Benjamin refused you a loan – and you took a chance. That realization you had as we spoke about your late-night trip to the bathroom upstairs. You told me that you were very drunk, and you stumbled around trying different doors to find first the bathroom and then your own room. I suspect one of the doors you tried was Barbara's – this is what disturbed you so during the night, you did not dream it after all. You tried another room as well before giving up and going back downstairs to sleep. What you didn't realize, in your drunken stupor, was that the second bedroom you entered belonged to Margaret. It only came back to you during our interview.'

'But I don't understand,' said Abigail. 'What does it matter if he went into Margaret's room by accident?'

'Yes, exactly,' said Margaret.

'It matters because the room he had stumbled into was empty. You had just come from the bathroom and so you knew Margaret was not there. And she was also not downstairs because you would have passed each other on the way. You realized that Margaret was not in her bedroom around the time that Benjamin was murdered.'

Declan couldn't seem to find the words. He looked defeated. Abigail cried out and Stephen put an arm around her.

'This is nonsense. Totally—tell them Declan—there is no way he could remember—he was so drunk—it would never hold—'

Bell turned to Margaret.

'You were in love with Benjamin, you were engaged to be married and then he broke it off. You pretended to be okay with it, that it was a joint decision but inside your heart burned red and angry. You were hurt and humiliated. And then before you both arrived at this house, he told you something – something about Barbara – that caused your heart to burst and anger and hatred to invade every part of your body. In the night, you went to Benjamin's room. Maybe to persuade him to return to you, perhaps just to argue, but he did not want to speak with you. And so you returned later when the occupants of this house were all asleep. And in an act of fury, you killed him. There are many bottles of poison located in the gardener's shed. And then in your room I found an empty bottle of expensive perfume—You sprayed your deadly poison as he slept, changed the time on the alarm clock and placed a bottle of sleeping pills on the nightstand. Then you left the room locking the door from the outside.'

Barbara put her hand to her mouth. Abigail cried out again. Stephen swore.

'But that doesn't make any sense,' said Cormac. 'The door

was locked, and the key was on the inside of the door when we checked on him the next morning.'

'Ah yes. The mystery of the locked door. Once the door had been kicked in, it would have taken nothing for Margaret to remove the key from her dressing gown pocket and slip it back into the lock while the rest of you were otherwise engaged. Likewise, taking a single earring from Barbara's jewellery box and planting it on the body for me to find was merely child's play.'

Bell turned to Declan now.

'I would advise you sir, whatever your debts, whatever your misfortunes, not to continue to provide a bogus alibi for a murderer. For that is what she is. Be a good friend to Benjamin, at last, even in death.'

Declan struggled to control his breathing. The room waited while he gathered himself.

'It is true—' he said eventually. 'She wasn't in her room—'

All hell broke loose then. Margaret ran at Bell, pushing him over to the floor and screaming until Cormac and Stephen pulled her off. Abigail was distraught. Barbara was catatonic. Sacker went to help Bell up.

'No, no. Leave me. Please go outside and get Inspector Ferret,' Bell said to Sacker. 'He is waiting at the bottom of the drive to arrest the suspect.'

Sacker did as he was told. Margaret was still screaming wildly. Cormac and Stephen were struggling to restrain her. Bell picked himself up gingerly and surveyed the group, who were a scene of devastation.

'Oh dear,' said Bell. 'Oh dear. Wrong again.'

*

She had never been to Cormac's house before – well, it was Cormac and Olivia's house now. They came as a pair. They were their own family. Their own unit. It is in a nice area of the city: very few cars, no loud voices, tall trees, a small shop on the corner selling homemade cakes. She walks past a house with a child's bicycle flung on the lawn and a cat stepping through the gaps in a cast-iron gate. Cormac and Olivia's house has a selection of gnarled gnomes in the front garden. Was this their style? Maybe they were gifts. Or had they already been there when they had moved in? It is so difficult to tell what people are really like. Cormac opens the door to her. He steps out and hugs her before welcoming her inside. Olivia peeks her head around the kitchen door to say a quick hello and to offer tea or coffee. She brings a hot kettle and some biscuits into the sitting room but then returns to the kitchen. Abigail can hear her typing on her laptop. She suspects they had discussed and planned this visit before her arrival. They are both playing their roles. It is a delicate balance. While Cormac pours the tea, Abigail allows her gaze to fall over the room and its objects. It is packed with things she would love to examine if she had the chance. 'How are you?' asks Cormac. 'Such a silly question, but I have to ask.' 'I'm fine,' says Abigail. 'I'm just very tired all the time . . . But I'm . . . I'm okay.' Cormac nods. 'And how are you?' Abigail asks. 'I'm tired too. And I feel . . . Olivia and I have been taking lots of long walks. And I read a lot and we watch a movie every night. I think it is helping somehow,' he says. 'I'm glad you came to visit.' 'Yes, I've been meaning to but . . .' 'No, no, no of course.' He opens the biscuit packet. 'How are things at work?' asks Cormac. 'Things are fine. I took some time off at the start of the year initially but now I'm back full-time.' 'It's good to get back into some sort of a routine,' he says. People love routines. People love normality. They all believe she needs to return to normality in order to move on. But it's really so that they can move on. She takes a sip of tea and picks up a biscuit that she knows she won't eat. 'I wanted to talk to you. About Benjamin,' she says. 'I want to know what you know. If you know anything. I feel . . . I feel that I've missed something and I'm hoping you can help me fill in some gaps.' Cormac looks at her with blank fear. 'I didn't know . . . if that's what you mean . . .' he says. 'I . . . I . . . It was a shock to me, of course.' Abigail interrupts him. 'But is there something I should know? Is there something that you noticed then, maybe you thought it was nothing and now you think differently about it? Was there something he said? I know that there are probably things he would tell you – a friend, a man – that he wouldn't tell me.' Cormac pauses for a moment. 'I have been thinking about this a lot. I was shocked. I just want to be clear about that. It was completely out of the blue. I had no idea what might have been . . . but there was only one thing I could think of. I remembered it one day when me and Olivia were talking, and I don't know whether it should be given any weight. It was a . . . And I don't know now whether it has any meaning in this context but . . . when we . . . it was after college. Maybe the year after. I think we were both working then, and we were on a night out, there were others there as well, a group of us. And we were drunk of course. I can't remember if it was someone's birthday. And we were walking home – we were in the habit of doing that in those days, walk home at three a.m. or whatever – and we were going over a bridge and he asked me if I had ever thought of just jumping off. He said that he had thought about it. And in my drunken state I didn't realize what he was saying to me. I said no, no of course not. I didn't understand. I think I laughed. We were all alone on the bridge. It was the way he said it too. Like it was nothing. Like it was a joke or . . . I think maybe it was around the time your dad . . . And it was days later that I remembered it. I just thought it was drunken nonsense – the kind of stupid thing you say when you've had a few too many but nothing serious. And to be honest even now I still think that. Even now I find it difficult to connect the two things.' 'He talked about throwing himself off a bridge, but you didn't think it was serious?' Abigail asks. 'Abigail, this was so many years ago. And things are said . . . on nights out. Other friends have . . . I'm probably not telling it right. I'm making it into a bigger thing than it was. I know how this sounds. But there were never any other signs. He never mentioned it again,' says Cormac. He starts to say something and then stops and then he starts again. 'If it happened now, I think my response would be different. I would have taken it in another way. I would have asked him about it. I would have checked in. Things are always more serious when you are a proper adult. We talked in such a flippant way then . . .' Cormac stops and calls out to Olivia. She comes to the door of the sitting room. 'Would you mind . . . Abigail and I are talking about what happened and maybe . . .' Olivia comes into the room and takes a seat on the sofa opposite them. Her hands are folded in her lap. She and Cormac share a look between them and then he says, 'When Olivia was a teenager, her uncle killed himself.' Cormac looks at her and Olivia slowly, tentatively takes over. 'No one ever talked about it. And I just thought growing up that that was normal and right and it was only a couple of years ago that I suddenly realized we should have been talking about it. I was quietly angry at everyone for a long time. I didn't understand why no one had stopped him. I didn't understand why he had done it. The whole thing seemed simple to me. And then I read an article about someone who had had suicidal feelings in the past. This man said that for him it was just a fleeting thought, just a momentary feeling. He had a plan in place one night, and then he received a phone call from a friend who was at a pub quiz and needed an answer to a question and he got distracted and then he didn't do it after all. He was still alive. And it threw me. I had assumed that my uncle had been planning this over a long period of time. Everything he had done in the previous months was parsed in the language and the context of his suicide. Everything he had said. Any plans he had cancelled. Any decisions he had made at work were, we thought, part of his path towards ending his life. They were clues to be gathered. But I realized that that probably wasn't true. That was probably just a story we were telling ourselves to make sense of what had happened.' They sit in silence then. Abigail is struggling to regulate her breathing. 'So,' she says eventually, 'Benjamin just decided there and then that that was the best thing to do? He didn't really . . .' Olivia interrupts her. 'I don't know. Is the truth. None of us do. I'm just providing you with my perspective and my understanding. Unfortunately, there won't be a neat ending here. I . . .' But Abigail has stood up. 'I'm going to go,' she says. She doesn't want to cry in front of them. Not again. She had promised herself. 'Oh,' says Cormac. 'Are you sure?' 'I didn't mean to upset you,' Olivia says. 'No, no, you didn't . . . I just . . .' Abigail walks herself to the front door and they follow her. She is full of humiliation and remorse. 'There was a book that a friend gave me to read,' says Olivia. 'She gave it to me to help me come to terms with my feelings. And it really did help me. I think you might find some solace in it. But please don't feel any pressure to read it straight away. Just put it by your bed and come to it when it feels right.' Abigail accepts the book, which feels like another weight to carry. 'And,' says Olivia, 'you can always talk to me. Or Cormac. I know you have a lot of people around you, and you don't know me that well but I'm here if you want to talk or whatever . . .' Abigail nods and thanks her. As she closes the gate at the bottom of the path, she turns slightly and sees them. Cormac is kissing Olivia's forehead and she is hugging his torso. Abigail wonders if she will ever see them again. There will be a wedding of course. She'll be invited to that. And everyone will be there. And Cormac will mention Benjamin in his speech. And life will have moved on. Sometime in the future she might pass them on the street, and they will be awkward with each other. She feels now as though she has been intruding on their domestic life and feels a deep aching badness for the sorrow she has brought to their doorstep.

Chapter Twenty-Five

ANOTHER SOLUTION

'Of course!' Bell declared suddenly. 'How could I have been such a fool!'

He called Sacker to him.

'Please, Sacker, gather everyone in the drawing room.'

'Have you found a solution?'

'Yes, I have. Just now. And I have been so stupid. I can't believe it. It was right in front of my eyes. Now, please, Sacker – do hurry. We can't waste any more time.'

Sacker went off to gather everyone. The household calmly and cautiously made their way to the drawing room as Bell had instructed. They were all dressed formally for dinner. Bell was there waiting, standing imperiously in front of them. The room bubbled silently with anticipation.

Once the door had closed heavily behind the last of them, he began.

'An odd feeling came over me suddenly in Chapter Three,' said Bell. 'I couldn't quite place it. It was a familiarity of sorts. I thought it might be this house. Maybe I had been here before. I have visited so many country houses during my career. I thought maybe the plot was familiar. Which in some ways it is, but still that did not satisfy the unsettling feeling I had. I realized just this morning what this feeling was. There is even a name for it: déjà vu. It is a loanword from French, and it means 'already seen'. That is it: I have already seen something in this house.' He paused. 'A face.'

Someone gasped. Others shuffled in their seats.

'I recognized somebody here. Not that big of a deal, you might say, and you would be correct. But this face does not bring me happy thoughts. It is the face of a murderer.'

'But that couldn't be,' said Abigail. 'It is just us here.'

'But surely, mademoiselle, you can see that you are wrong. This is a murder mystery, correct? And so, someone here must be a murderer.'

'Well, tell us who it is then,' said Declan, who was standing with his hands stuffed tightly into his pockets.

'Not quite yet, Declan. I need to set the scene,' said Bell. 'I have been thinking a lot about the past. I have become a little obsessed, if I'm being honest. My mind keeps returning to my previous adventures. In fact, one case in particular: my first one. It was over thirty years ago now. I solved a murder which made me famous and set me off on this second career of detecting. I have recently been giving thought to retiring. A thought which I had not shared with anyone – not even Sacker. And I had assumed that my mind kept returning to my first case for this very reason. But no – that was not what my brain was doing. In fact, my brain was trying to tell me something, something very important, but stupidly I ignored it.'

Bell started to pace the room.

'This case had too many clues. Too many red herrings. Too many suspects. Too many motives. From the beginning it

seemed like something was off. This wasn't simply a murder.
This was a murder that was masquerading as something else,
just like someone here is masquerading as some*one* else.'

'Mr Bell,' said Abigail. 'You're confusing me. What does all
this mean?'

Bell turned to her and said, 'I will make it very simple. The
murderer is here in this room. And this murderer is pretend-
ing to be someone they are not.'

'Well, who is it then?' asked Stephen, a frustrated tone in
his voice.

Bell turned.

'It is – Olivia.'

Cormac stood immediately, outrage on his face. Olivia did
not move an inch.

'Oh my god, did she do it? Did she kill Benjamin?' cried
Margaret.

'Of course not, don't be stupid,' said Cormac. Olivia, still
seated, was clasping her own shaking hands.

'Well, that seems to be what Bell is saying,' said Stephen.
He was eyeing Olivia warily.

'Quite a long time ago, I was involved in a famous case. It
has been a long time since then, but I would never forget the
face of the first murderer I had ever come across. That is the
face I see before me.'

The others didn't know what to say.

'I suspect that you have changed your name? And your hair
colour as well. You look so much like your mother, though; it
is hard to disguise oneself completely.'

Olivia, through tears, nodded her head.

'Look here,' Cormac said. 'Is there any need for this? Olivia never knew her mother. She was taken from her after she gave birth in prison. This is harassment.'

'You knew about this?' said Margaret.

'Of course,' Cormac said. 'We're planning on getting married. But what difference does it make? Are we all to be judged by the sins of our parents?'

'Bad blood, old boy,' sniffed Declan. Cormac, without hesitation, got up from his chair, strode across the room and punched Declan straight in the face. Nobody stopped him. Declan reeled back but didn't retaliate.

Cormac turned to Bell pleadingly. 'Please, you can't think— I mean, what would be the motive?'

'I think,' said Bell, 'that Benjamin had found out about her past and was threatening to tell. I found this in a locked drawer in his office.' He revealed the date book with its scribbled words. 'I thought the case was haunting me, but now I realize I have been haunting it. I didn't realize what these words meant earlier, but now I do. Benjamin knew your secret and he was also in dire need of cash.' He turned to Olivia. 'And he was blackmailing you.'

'It was me,' said Cormac, suddenly rushing to the centre of the room. 'I did it.'

Everyone gasped. Abigail tried to stand up, but her legs wobbled beneath her. Stephen held on to her arm.

'You? Cormac?' Abigail had to sit down again and then she erupted into tears.

'I had an argument with Benjamin in his room after we went to bed and— I had gone to try to sort out this whole business. Man to man. I thought he would see sense. I told him that I was planning to marry Olivia. We wanted to begin a new life together. A new start. Free from all this nonsense. We were going to move abroad – but he just wouldn't listen. He was being so unreasonable and so I lashed out. I hit him and hit him again and then he fell back, and his head hit the side of the bed. And he stopped moving. Oh god – I panicked. I knew how it looked even though of course it was an accident. But I knew no one would believe me.' He retook his seat then and wrapped an arm around his fiancée. 'I am so sorry. I wish I could take it back.' His voice was just a whisper now.

'Well, that's that then,' said Stephen. 'A terrible accident. We've all known Cormac for years. I know he couldn't have done this on purpose.'

'Is that your conclusion too?' asked Margaret.

'Not exactly,' said Bell.

'But I swear to you it was an accident,' said Cormac.

'Oh yes, absolutely. I believe what you say. But I do not believe that you are the one who killed Benjamin.'

'What do you mean?' asked Abigail.

'I think, Cormac,' continued Bell, 'that you returned to your bedroom and confessed all to your intended wife. You were heartbroken, of course, and she comforted you. But she was not heartbroken. She has no connection, no familiar feelings for Benjamin. She wanted him dead. That is the truth. But she needed to make sure that he was dead, and that Cormac had not left anything incriminating in the room. She returned later that night after Cormac had gone to sleep in order to set the scene: her plan was to lock the door from the inside, and then leave the balcony door open so it would appear that the killer came from outside. But unfortunately, Olivia found Benjamin coming to from his unconscious state.

He was not dead, just greatly concussed. Now, Olivia has a choice to make: does she leave the room, allowing Benjamin to call out for help? That would lead to him naming Cormac as his attacker, which would lead to Cormac being ostracized from the rest of the group and possibly worse. And of course, Benjamin would still reveal her true identity. It would be the end of them. No, this was not an option for the quick-thinking Olivia. Instead, she took what she felt was the only other option: she decided to finish the job herself. A pillow, was it? It probably wasn't very difficult with him in that state.

'And then you arranged the body so that it looked like a suicide before leaving via the balcony – you will recall that she had been a champion gymnast in her youth. In our experiment, we looked at how difficult it would be for one to enter the room from the balcony, but of course we failed to see how easy it would be to exit via that same route. This was the thump you heard in the night, Abigail. She let herself into the house via the side door and went upstairs again.'

'No, no,' said Cormac quietly.

'She had so much to lose if Benjamin regained consciousness,' said Bell. 'She felt it had to be done.'

'I did it for us!' exclaimed Olivia. 'I was afraid that if he came to he would identify you as his attacker and me as a murderer's daughter. Though, of course, I have become a murderer now. Maybe he was right about me.'

'You should have allowed me to take the blame,' Cormac cried. The others were silent, unable to process what they had just been told.

*

'A sorry state of affairs,' said Bell to Ferret as Cormac and Olivia were led out to the waiting police van.

'Do you genuinely feel sorry for them?' asked Ferret.

'I can't help but pity them. Such a mess. They assumed that no one would have stood by them. That the force of Benjamin would have turned everyone against them. And maybe they were right.'

'Murder is still murder,' said Ferret.

'Indeed. She will be sent to the gallows, I suppose,' said Bell.

'Yes, and he will spend a long time in prison for assault and any other charges we can get to stick.'

'Is that everything?' asked Ferret.

'Not quite,' replied Bell.

*

Abigail had forgotten about Barbara. It was terrible to admit that. And then once she had remembered her, she felt awkward about reaching out. Too much time had passed. But she was curious. She wondered what had happened when Barbara had gone back to work in January. What questions did people ask? What did she tell them? And she wondered about things long before that too. Work was the one area of her brother's life that she had never had access to. He talked about promotions and skites and team-building exercises and she would nod in a supportive sort of way, but she never really paid attention. When she did eventually contact Barbara via her work email Barbara had suggested meeting in a coffee place in town. She shared a house with two others, and she didn't think they would be able to talk privately. Abigail thought nothing of it at the time but now, sitting and waiting with a flat white, she thought about how little she knew about Barbara and how this coffee date created another kind of distance between them. She would have liked to see how Barbara lived, liked to see what books she owned and whether she was inherently tidy or messy. Barbara is apologetic when she arrives; her meeting had run long. She is a little flustered.

Abigail asks her about work and Barbara sighs and says, 'busy, busy' but she doesn't want to dwell on it. Abigail wonders if they could be friends. It is an odd situation they are both in. Flung together by circumstance. Abigail engages a little in some small talk while they are waiting for Barbara's coffee to arrive. It is a stilted and one-sided affair with Abigail unusually doing most of the talking. Barbara looks tense in her seat. 'Could I ask you some questions?' Abigail asks eventually and Barbara relaxes. 'Of course,' she says. 'What was Benjamin like at work?' 'Oh. He was a good employee – and a good co-worker, which aren't necessarily the same thing. He was well liked by everyone. Easy-going. I know these sound like platitudes but it's the truth. He was just good at everything. Good with the work and good with people too. I'm not, so I value it in others.' Barbara pauses then. 'Benjamin and I had our desks next to each other, so that's how we became friends. I've had a weird year. My fiancé, well, not fiancé anymore . . . and I think he took pity on me. That's why he invited me to his birthday . . .' 'Benjamin didn't take pity on anyone. He didn't do things for the sake of politeness,' Abigail says. 'He invited you because he liked you.' Barbara's face brightens gently. 'Did you . . . in some ways you were with him for more of the week than any of us . . . did you notice anything? See anything?' 'No.' Barbara shakes her head. 'I've thought a lot about this. I've gone over it a lot. And there was nothing. He seemed totally fine, always. And he . . . he noticed it in other people. When anyone at work was suffering or having a hard time or whatever. He noticed it in me. He was good at spotting the signs. That's the funny thing.' 'I've been trying to piece everything together,' says Abigail. 'It doesn't make sense to me. I've been asking everyone. I want to see if I missed anything.' 'I understand,' says Barbara. 'Work has offered me free counselling sessions. I've gone to one so far. I'm not sure if it's helping yet but it's been good to say things out loud. There was an empty desk next to mine for the first two weeks back and then someone moved in, and it was . . . I didn't realize it would affect me so much. We miss him. At work. We all miss him so much. They say that it can be a year before someone is able to truly grieve for their deceased partner. I can imagine you being in the same situation.' 'A year,' Abigail says. 'That seems like such a long time.' She wonders what next Christmas will be like. Next New Year's. After their mother died, Christmas became so much smaller and after their father died, she and Benjamin had had to reinvent it for themselves. They had made a conscious effort to create new traditions and to let go of what didn't work anymore. Friends would invite them over, but they would always say no. And she loved these new Christmases because they had made them quietly and carefully theirs. She brings her coffee mug to her mouth to hide her trembling lip. Behind Barbara, she can see a family – a man, a woman and two small girls. The two girls have pancakes piled up on their plates. Their father tries to help by cutting them into bitesize pieces, but the two girls insist on doing it themselves. They struggle with the cutlery and the size of the giant pancakes, and their parents are laughing. People trail in and out to get takeaway coffees and cake. Others are leaning against the ledge outside talking on their phones, getting a little of the early sun. Barbara asks about everyone else. She doesn't know them, of course. She is very much on the outside, but she is just being polite. Abigail doesn't really know what to say. She realizes that she is on the outside now as well. They are all Benjamin's friends, after all. 'What happened with your fiancé?' asks Abigail suddenly and then she stops herself. 'I'm sorry. I'm not thinking. I'm a little bit more blunt than usual.' 'No,' says Barbara. 'I don't mind. In fact, I enjoy bluntness. No one ever asks me about what happened. Like they don't ask me about Benjamin. It's all whispers and pats on the back. The truth is, or, well, the story that I have is that he just stopped loving me. I think the reality is a little bit more complicated.' 'Was he seeing someone else?' 'I don't think so. Funnily enough, I think that would have made it easier. There's a familiarity to that story that would have been – god this is an odd word to use – but comforting. If that makes sense. But . . . it doesn't matter now. I mean it really doesn't matter now. I was sad about it for a long time and then it suddenly became insignificant. Now I have some clarity on the whole thing. I have a rich and full life. I hope you get there too. And that you have support around you. All those friends. It's good to have that group.' Abigail thought she might cry. They walk out together. 'I'm parked over here,' says Barbara and they walk towards her car. 'I'm glad you called now. Well, it's just . . . I wasn't sure. You don't really know me but . . . I'm glad you called, and we could talk about this.' The way she said it sounded very final, as if this whole thing could be wrapped up in one conversation. They're at her car and Barbara hesitates. 'I'm sorry I didn't have any answers for you,' she says. 'That's okay. I'm not sure what I was expecting.' 'I have this . . .' Barbara gestures at the back seat. She unlocks the car, opens the back door and takes out a small box. 'I'm not sure . . . You don't have to take it . . .' Abigail opens the box and inside she can see some photographs, some figurine she doesn't recognize, a few reams of stationery and she realizes that this is the contents of Benjamin's desk. They say their goodbyes and Abigail walks to the bus stop feeling as though she is carrying her brother's ashes.

*

While on the bus she receives a call from her Garda liaison officer. He tells her that she can come and collect Benjamin's phone whenever it suits her. She had completely forgotten about the phone. It was so silly. Why had she been thinking about a diary? The phone is the thing. She tells the Garda that she is on her way. She gets off at the next stop and walks through the city centre, box in hand, to the station. It was like it was meant to be. She forces that thought all the way down. She doesn't believe in fate. She waits patiently as the Garda on duty helps two people fill in a passport application form. Eventually, she is at the counter. After she explains why she is there, the Garda's posture immediately changes. He becomes softer. The phone is handed to her in a plastic bag, and he tells her gently to have a nice weekend. She puts it inside the box and manages to hold out until she gets home. Once there, she drops the box onto the floor and removes the plastic bag. Her hand dips in and she removes the phone. It still has some battery; they must have charged it at the station. She swipes up and sees the words 'Face ID'. When the phone doesn't recognize her, she is shown a screen prompting her to enter a passcode. She thinks for just a moment and then keys in the first series of six numbers she thinks of. The phone unlocks. Fate again. She sits on the wooden floor, the box in front of her, one foot stuck underneath herself uncomfortably and she goes through his phone: photographs of a cute dog on the train, his to-do lists, messages between him and a woman on Tinder that peter out from November, unread newsletters in his email inbox, the long list of notifications about football scores and breaking political news, an alert that he has not backed up his phone in twenty weeks, open browser windows: a *New York Times* article, Wordle, a Google search result page for quicksand. She looks through apps, and spots Instagram. She didn't think Benjamin had any social media. She opens it up and starts scrolling through his feed: it's a mishmash of exotic locations, food, and a handful of famous people. There are only twelve photographs on his grid: all arty and mysterious. She recognizes a plant from his flat. None of this seems like him at all. She goes into each photograph and analyzes every comment and like. He doesn't seem to be followed by anyone she knows. He is completely anonymous. There are no DMs or follower requests. Then so many text messages between herself and him. It is so odd to see yourself on the other side of the conversation. She scrolls back and back reading through their messages together. The most recent one: *Will you be here soon?* He hadn't replied. He hadn't needed to. He arrived at the house just ten minutes later.

Chapter Twenty-Six

AND ANOTHER

'Of course!' Bell declared suddenly. 'How could I have been such a fool!'

He called Sacker to him.

'Please, Sacker, gather everyone in the drawing room.'

'Have you found a solution?'

'Yes, I have. Just now. And I have been so stupid. I can't believe it. It was right in front of my eyes. Now, please, Sacker – do hurry. We can't waste any more time.'

Sacker went off to gather everyone. The household warily made their way to the drawing room as Bell had instructed. They were all dressed formally for dinner. Bell was there waiting, standing imperiously in front of them. The room bubbled silently with anticipation.

Once the door had closed heavily behind the last of them, he began.

'Murder is a straightforward crime,' he said, pacing back and forth slowly. 'That might seem reductive, but in my vast experience it holds true. Of course, in this situation we have an added complication – a trope in murder mysteries – of an outside threat. A b-story that runs alongside the a-story, always threatening to take over but ultimately continuing to run parallel. Two rails never touching. And now Detective Inspector Ferret, who by the way is waiting outside with some of his men, has provided me with certain information that has been very enlightening. The murderer was very clever. And the method of murder was ingenious.

'Abigail, when you spoke to me originally you told me, perhaps without knowing, that you were not as flush with cash as you once were. And this was confirmed by Dorcas, the maid, who talked about the downsizing of the staff. "Things change," she said. Even those charming people at the inn were aware that you were both under some financial pressure. Your neighbours had been approached by Benjamin about buying some land and of course, Declan had his loan refused. I think you assumed that Benjamin had finally had enough of you, Declan, and indeed while that could well be correct, I believe a forensic investigation of the accounts will show that Benjamin did not have the means to provide you with another loan.'

Bell paused there to allow everyone to take this in. Then he continued his pacing of the room.

'So, what does this young man do? He has a house and an estate to run. He has a family business that is faltering. He has his good name and reputation to uphold. Well, he needs a way to make money and quickly. Early on, I am visited by Detective Inspector Ferret, who tells me about a jewellery-smuggling ring who are working in the area and who use big houses as a front for their criminal enterprises. Of course, it makes sense. It is an excellent plan. No police officer would ever search a house like this. It is perfect. The place is practically off-limits. But of course, Benjamin would need to have a partner. Someone who worked as a link between himself and the gang.'

Bell finally stopped in front of Barbara.

'I knew it. I knew it,' declared Margaret triumphantly.

'You may have had your suspicions, Margaret, but they were not accurate. Barbara was not in a relationship with Benjamin. They were not in love. Not even friends, I suspect. They were partners in crime. That is all.'

'No, no, that doesn't make sense,' said Abigail. 'My brother would never have involved himself in something like that.'

Bell spoke to her in a kind manner.

'I know how difficult this is. But I also don't think you understand how much pressure your brother was under and what people do when put in this situation. If it is any great comfort to you, he did this to protect you.'

Barbara had still not said a word.

'This is a case of absences. When I checked your room, Barbara, I noticed many absences – few clothes in your wardrobe besides what you had worn the night before – a sure sign that you didn't intend to spend any further time here. This is the type of house where everyone dresses for breakfast each day, never mind dinner or drinks or shooting. And yet you had one evening dress and one daytime dress and one coat and that was it.'

Barbara sat resolutely.

'And then your jewellery box with a single set of pearls – quite beautiful – and one set of diamond earrings. But then when I presented you with the earring found in Benjamin's room you said it was yours. If that was the truth, mademoiselle, then its fellow should have resided in your jewellery box waiting to be reunited with its partner. And yet . . .'

Barbara still said nothing.

'Earlier on in this case, I did believe the theory that you were having an affair with Benjamin. Indeed, I think you played this up to mislead me. But yet again I saw an absence – this time an absence of sadness. You have never seemed overly upset about the death of your dear kind employer or your lover or your friend – whatever pretence we were to believe. But that's because you weren't sad at all. You had no need to be. You had no connection to this man outside of your criminal partnership –' Bell raised his hands to the ceiling – 'Absences,' he said simply.

Olivia had begun crying a little, and Cormac was comforting her. Abigail and Stephen looked shocked and unable to move. Margaret was looking triumphant.

'So how did she do it then?' Declan asked, somewhat confused.

Bell raised a single finger. 'Ah, that is the ingenious part of things. And another absence in this case. A violent death and yet no murder weapon. When looking at the autopsy report, something stood out to me. A small observation made by the doctor but intriguing nonetheless: when he initially examined the body in the bedroom, the doctor noted that the deceased's pyjama top was damp. He didn't think anything of it because his focus was on the empty bottle of sleeping pills, but I paid attention. In Chapter One, I noticed an absence – a space – where the shotguns were mounted on the landing of the stairs and then in Chapter Fifteen suddenly that space had been filled – by a crossbow. And I am reminded of *Cleek of Scotland Yard* by Thomas W. Hanshew, or *Initials Only* by Anna Katherine Green. An icicle fired from a crossbow through the open balcony door. You lure Benjamin to the balcony, he is struck by the projectile, staggers back and dies. And then the icicle melts – just disappears. Another absence.'

'And you knew this from the start?' asked Abigail.

'I knew the method, or at least I had a good idea about the method. But I did not know for sure that Barbara was the murderer until my good friend the detective inspector confirmed my suspicions after the arrest of her fellow criminals. Then I recalled the single gold earring I found on Benjamin, and everything fell into place.'

'What do you have to say for yourself?' Stephen asked Barbara.

'How are you going to weasel your way out of this one?' asked Margaret.

Barbara stood slowly and said gently, 'Good night,' before beginning to stride towards the drawing room door.

'Grab her,' yelled Margaret. 'Stop her. Why aren't you doing anything?'

'There is no need for that,' Bell said. 'Ferret and his men are stationed outside. There is nowhere for you to go, Barbara. This is the end of the line.'

Barbara hesitated. Finally, her cool demeanour left her.

'I had no choice,' she said. 'Benjamin chickened out at the last moment, leaving me in the lurch. This wasn't just about him. This was about me as well. I don't have money like the rest of you. This was going to be my ticket out of here to a new life. And then . . . well, you can't depend on a man. I should have known. He was about to betray me.'

'Ah yes, the note you read in his date book when you were making a phone call from his office,' said Bell. 'You believed he was going to the authorities and that would be the end for you and your associates.'

'Benjamin knew too much. Even if he hadn't phoned them, I would have been looking over my shoulder for the rest of my life. He was a spiteful bastard when it came down to it.'

Abigail cried out but Barbara just shrugged.

'It's just the truth. That's what you were looking for, wasn't it? The truth. Well, now you have it. The whole unvarnished mess of it.'

'Sacker, I think you can call the detective inspector in now,' Bell said.

'I suppose it's the gallows for me,' said Barbara without emotion.

'I think you are much too smart for that,' said Bell.

*

'Will she hang?' asked Sacker, as Barbara was taken to the waiting police car.

'I suspect she will do a deal – she is only one cog in a large criminal enterprise. She has some cards up her sleeve yet.'

'I'm amazed by you, Bell,' said Sacker. 'I never would have guessed. And you have remained so cool and calm. You seem completely unruffled by the evening's dramatic events.'

But Bell was still thinking.

*

Declan's mother had made a sponge cake which was too sweet and a little dry, but Abigail ate it all the same. She had known this woman for as long as she had had a memory, though their relationship had never been close. She was one of those adults in Abigail's life who was always at a distance. As a child, she had thought Declan's home hopelessly old fashioned: all florals and knick-knacks and his mother with her perm. They didn't have satellite television and they had tea in the evening, not dinner. Now, two decades later, the house is exactly the same: preserved in time. She wonders what age Declan's mother is: she couldn't be anything older than early seventies, but she has seemed about eighty-five for the past thirty years. As Abigail sits there eating dry sponge cake and drinking raspberry cordial out of a plastic picnic glass, she wonders why she had never thought about Declan's father. It had always been just him and his mother, and Declan had never mentioned him. Benjamin probably knew. It made her think differently of the tiny woman in front of her cleaning cream off her cardigan. She had raised Declan by herself. He is her pride and joy. Of course he is. She had spoiled him but that is understandable, and it makes Abigail feel a little bit more generous towards Declan. Declan's mother starts talking about a television show she likes. She asks Abigail if she's watching it too, but she isn't. Declan's mother talks about it anyway: the presenter she likes, the other presenter she isn't sure about because he reminds her of someone whose name she can't remember, all the little things about the show that annoy her, how there's too much on television now and how she would recommend Abigail watch it anyway. Declan just continues to eat his slice of cake in silence. She wonders what Declan's mother used to do when Declan was at theirs all the time. As a child he would have dinner with them more than once a week. Was she eating by herself? Watching television by herself? Did she work during the day? And now, of course, she can't get rid of him. Declan would say that he still lives at home because he was helping her out or that he was saving money for a deposit, but Abigail suspects that he just likes it too much. She realizes that she is a little bit worried about Declan. Benjamin was his one real friend. There is no partner and there has never been anyone who had stuck around long enough. She's never heard of him being involved in any hobbies. Does he have any work friends? If she is being honest, she can't even remember what he does for a living. Benjamin seemed to think that he earned good money, but she isn't sure where he got that idea from. She can't imagine Declan at work. She can't imagine Declan at anything. Does he listen to music? Does he like football? Abigail's eyes wander around the room and rest on the mantelpiece covered with precious objects: a marble clock, a bunch of postcards, ceramic animals, and a small gold picture frame with a photo of Declan and Benjamin as children. Declan's mother tells Abigail that the funeral was lovely, but she wonders why it was private. 'I know it was your choice but there's just something about a private funeral,' she says. 'It's a little bit cold. That's no judgement, of course. And no church? I mean, I know you're not churchgoers, but it would have been so nice to have a blessing – I could say something to Father Flynn and we could have a late month's mind if you like. It's no bother.' Declan's mother assumed everyone was a Catholic but that some people were just secretive about it. 'No month's mind. We might do something in the future but not right now. There's the inquest that I—' 'An inquest?' says Declan. The first thing he has said all afternoon. 'Yes,' says Abigail. 'They have to . . . I think it's going to be routine. That's what they tell me. I'm surprised you haven't received a witness summons.' Declan looks confused. 'Well, that letter did come for you . . .' his mother says, and Declan raises his eyes to the ceiling. He puts down his plate of cake and goes to the hallway. Nearly immediately he returns with a white envelope. 'Mother . . .' He sits there and reads the short letter silently to himself and then slides it back into the envelope. 'Okay then,' he says more to himself than anyone else. Abigail wants to speak to him alone, but she isn't sure she will get the opportunity. She is also unsure as to whether he will be able to help her. She is realizing rather belatedly that there is not going to be some jolt, some brightening of the skies, some awakening of the mind. There will never really be clarity again. There will just be this fug. Instead, she asks Declan's mother about her garden and that sets her off on the weather and the cost of petunias. The good thing about Declan's mother is that you never have to think of things to say. 'Do you want to stay for tea, darling?' Declan's mother asks. 'Oh, no thank you,' Abigail says, taking this as her cue to leave. 'Do you have your car with you?' 'I'll just walk to the bus stop,' Abigail says. 'Oh, no, we can't have that. Declan will drive you home.' 'Oh, that's okay, don't worry . . .' Abigail starts to say, but Declan has already gone out to the hallway to get his keys. 'C'mon,' he says to her and doesn't wait for her to respond. He goes out and sits in the car and starts the engine. Abigail thanks Declan's mother for everything and collects her jacket and bag. 'And remember,' says Declan's mother, 'you are always welcome here. Always.' She gets into the car with Declan, who starts the engine and backs out of the driveway. Now that they are alone, Abigail doesn't know how to start. She doesn't really want to talk around it, but it is still difficult to approach it head-on. How many of these conversations will she have to go through? She will never get used to it. They sit in silence for a while. The radio is on low. 'So, will you be at the inquest?' she asks eventually. 'I suppose I have to be,' Declan says. 'I've been summoned.' He sniffs. 'Do you know what you'll say?' Abigail asks tentatively. Declan indicates and makes a right turn. 'What I'll say . . . I'll be saying the same thing I said to the Guards that morning and what I've said to them since and what I said to my mother and to anyone else who has asked me. I won't be saying anything that would shock you.' 'But . . .' Abigail powers through. '. . . it won't just be questions about that night. They'll want to know about anything that happened before.' Declan's eyes are on the road, but his face is scrunched-up. 'What do you mean?' he asks. 'I mean, they'll want to know if he had attempted suicide before . . .' 'Oh . . .' '. . . or if he was depressed or if he had said anything . . .' 'Had he said something to you?' Declan asks. 'No, no. That's the thing. He never said anything. Did he say anything to you?' 'No, of course not. I already told the Guards that.' There is a long silence while they wait at a red light. Two pedestrians hurry across the road. 'Had he tried to kill himself before?' asks Declan quietly. His hands are tightly gripping the steering wheel. 'No,' says Abigail. 'No, never. Why are you asking that?' Declan releases the handbrake, and the car moves forward once again. 'It's just the way you said it then. You made it sound like he had done something.' Abigail is staring straight ahead at the road. 'No,' she says. 'Never. If anything had happened, you would have known. You of all people.' 'I would hope so,' he says. Abigail is massaging her palm. 'We've both known him the longest and we didn't know . . .' 'A moment of madness,' says Declan. 'We could have stopped it,' she says. 'Maybe,' Declan replies, and he indicates into Abigail's drive and parks the car. 'But we didn't. And we don't have a time machine to go back and change things. Things are what they are.' The tears are coming now. 'If we . . . If I . . . He could have had such a nice long life.' 'I think that's the wrong way of thinking about it,' says Declan. 'He had a nice life. A lot of hard times, of course. But I have a lifetime of good memories because of him. You do too. That's what I focus on.' Abigail opens the car door. 'Will we still be friends?' she asks. 'If you want to be,' says Declan. 'Were we friends to begin with?' 'Well, you're Benjamin's friend and now . . . it would be odd if we suddenly didn't see each other.' 'My mother would be happy to have you over for Sunday lunch, that kind of thing,' he says. 'That would be nice.' Abigail pauses, her feet on the ground. 'Are you okay, Declan? I mean, will you be okay?' 'I suppose I'll just have to be,' he replies.

Chapter Twenty-Seven

AND ANOTHER

'Of course!' Bell declared suddenly. 'How could I have been such a fool!'

He called Sacker to him.

'Please, Sacker, gather everyone in the drawing room.'

'Have you found a solution?'

'Yes, I have. Just now. And I have been so stupid. I can't believe it. It was right in front of my eyes. Now, please, Sacker – do hurry. We can't waste any more time.'

Sacker went off to gather everyone. The household slowly and wearily made their way to the drawing room as Bell had instructed. They were all dressed formally for dinner. Bell was there waiting, standing imperiously in front of them. The room bubbled silently with anticipation.

Once the door had closed heavily behind the last of them, he began.

'I have to admit to being a little bit naive, a little, what will I say, obtuse. I thought that this was a difficult case. I thought that it was going to take all my experience to solve, but the solution was staring me in the face.

'So many of the murders I have previously investigated were committed for the simple motive of gain. What can be gained by this murder, or rather, who gains? And of course, when we think of gain, we think first of money. It is clear that Abigail would gain as the primary inheritor under her brother's will. But she is taken care of well enough and so I cannot see a motive in that regard for her. Of the others, there is only one who would gain financially from Benjamin's death. Only one person who had a motive and who has acknowledged a financial debt.'

The room as a whole turned towards Declan.

'Oh, calm down everybody,' Declan said. 'Haven't you ever read one of these things before? He'll go around the whole room before finding the killer. It isn't me.'

'It's true though that you had debts, Declan,' Cormac said.

'You're the only person with a motive,' said Margaret.

'Well, that's clearly not true, darling. You know that,' Declan said.

'What does that mean?' asked Margaret defiantly.

'You know exactly what it means,' replied Declan.

Bell intervened before things could get more heated.

'What you are discussing is a moot point. Everyone here has a motive. Everyone has been a suspect at one point or another. But not anymore. Now, I have my murderer,' said Bell. They all sobered up very quickly.

'I've been completely up front with my difficulties. I told you,' Declan said to Bell. 'I told you exactly what was going on.'

'Well, that is simply not true, Declan,' replied Bell, and Declan made an argumentative noise.

'You, sir,' continued Bell, 'were heard arguing with Benjamin about money. You admitted to me that you had racked up gambling debts and that Benjamin had bailed you out on more than one occasion. You had turned to him again looking for a small loan to tide you over, but he refused you. You told me all this to appear like an honest chap. Someone who was open and aware of his own faults. And yet you tried to deceive me. Yes, you argued over money, but you omitted the other thing you argued over. Benjamin had decided to cut you off completely. That included removing you from his will. That note in his date book – "ring FWC" – he was planning on phoning his solicitors, Freeman, Wills, Croft and Associates. And so, you knew that if you wished to benefit from your friend's estate, you would need to kill him before he had time to return to town to draw up a new will.'

Declan snorted with derision.

'You pretended to be drunk and to fall asleep on the sofa. You waited until the time was right and then you crept upstairs while everyone was asleep. In cold blood you murdered your one true friend with a single blow of a champagne bottle which you then threw off the balcony before arranging the body so that it looked as though Benjamin had taken his own life. Then you quietly closed the door behind you, locking it from the outside using the pliers you had stolen from the gardener's shed – not the screwdriver that Dorcas had also seen was missing. It was almost the perfect crime. The only evidence you left behind were the nearly imperceptible marks on the pin of the key. You went downstairs, fell asleep and pretended like nothing had happened.'

'Pure fantasy,' Declan said, rising from his seat. 'And if you've quite finished, I don't think I'll be sticking around for any more of this slander.'

'No sir, you will stay here and wait for the police if you are any kind of a man,' said Bell. Declan pushed his way past Bell easily and started towards the door, but Stephen blocked him.

'Get out of my way, Steve,' Declan snarled.

'I think it's better if you stay here a while,' Stephen replied. Declan pushed him hard, causing Stephen to stumble backwards, before moving quickly out of the drawing room and towards the front door. Abigail went to Stephen while Margaret and Cormac raced after Declan. Sacker followed them. They could hear shouting and banging outside and then a car engine roared. Sacker ran back into the drawing room.

'He's getting away in his race car,' he exclaimed.

'He won't get far,' Bell said. 'Remember, he is essentially penniless now. He has very few opportunities.'

Just then, they heard a loud bang in the distance, and they all rushed outside. From the front of the house, they could see a car on its side at the bottom of the driveway near the large, gated entrance. Its lights were on, and the engine was still running, but there was no movement.

Cormac raced down the driveway to the car. They watched as he removed his dinner jacket, wrapped it around his arm and then broke the window with his elbow. He was able to open the door from the inside, and then he dragged Declan out of the car. Olivia ran to him, and Margaret followed. But it was clear that they were all looking at a dead body.

'Not the ending you were hoping for,' said Sacker.

'What ending was I hoping for?' asked Bell.

*

Abigail phones her aunt and suggests that they should go for brunch some weekend. Her aunt doesn't want a fuss, but she ploughs on and books a table for the two of them at a small local cafe. Her aunt orders some toast and two sausages, and Abigail has the eggs Florentine. 'I've never been here before, it's very nice,' says her aunt. 'Very stylish.' 'We could set up a regular thing,' Abigail says. 'A lunch date or coffee or whatever suits you.' Her aunt says that would be nice. Abigail hadn't seen her aunt much over the last few years and she is feeling bad for that now. When you are in your twenties you don't really think about extended family in that way. It is less important to you. Especially, as in Abigail and Benjamin's case, when they had to create a new family of their own. 'I've been thinking about taking a break from work,' Abigail says. 'A long break. A semi-permanent one. Do a bit of travelling or something.' 'Maybe you need a change of scenery,' her aunt says. 'Travel is good for the soul. Go abroad and live and work there. Have adventures.' 'Have you had many adventures?' asks Abigail. 'Oh, my whole life has been adventures,' says her aunt. When she was a child, her aunt had lived in London but had returned home after Abigail's mother died. Before that she had lived in Morocco and Australia and Chicago. 'There's a big world out there,' says her aunt. 'Don't think you have to stay here for my sake. This is your opportunity to be selfish.' The waitress brings their plates of food and Abigail is glad that she can stuff food in her mouth and not speak for a while. If she did, her voice would give her away. Her aunt has never asked her to stay here. Has never expressed sadness at the thought of her going away. Would never make her feel guilty. She only wants what is best for her, and Abigail realizes that the only thing keeping her here is herself. 'I'm worried,' Abigail says. 'I'm worried I will never get over this.' Her aunt looks up at her. 'I don't think it's a case of getting over it. No one would ever expect you to get over it.' 'But how will I ever be able to move on?' ask Abigail. 'By living,' her aunt says. 'By living every day of your life. By taking tiny footsteps forward. Right now, it might seem impossible, but those footsteps accumulate. You will surprise yourself.' Abigail swallows. Her shoulders are hunched. 'I feel that I can't move forward without understanding what happened,' she says. 'I still haven't got any answers.' 'Well, maybe those answers will come. With time. Maybe you'll gain an understanding. And also, maybe you won't. You shouldn't allow that to dictate what happens from here on in. It's time to re-engage with the world. You've been hiding under the duvet a little too long.' Abigail is staring at her plate of food. 'I'm angry at him,' she says. Her voice is just a whisper. 'I'm angry at him for leaving me like this.' Her aunt reaches across the table to hold her wrist and they sit there like that until their coffees go cold. After their plates are cleared, her aunt says she has a couple of jobs to do around town and Abigail asks if she can join her. They go to the bank to cash a cheque and to Easons for a magazine and to the butcher's for pork chops and to the post office for an international stamp and to the florist for some flowers for a sick friend and to the pharmacy to collect a prescription. Abigail feels relaxed for the first time in months. In fact, she feels like a child again.

Chapter Twenty-Eight

AND THEN ONE MORE

'Of course!' Bell declared suddenly. 'How could I have been such a fool!'

He called Sacker to him.

'Please, Sacker, gather everyone in the drawing room.'

'Have you found a solution?'

'Yes, I have. Just now. And I have been so stupid. I can't believe it. It was right in front of my eyes. Now, please, Sacker – do hurry. We can't waste any more time.'

Sacker went off to gather everyone. The household reluctantly made their way to the drawing room as Bell had instructed. They were all dressed formally for dinner. Bell was there waiting, standing imperiously in front of them. The room bubbled silently with anticipation.

Once the door had closed heavily behind the last of them, he began.

'I have in the last few days had my mind twisted and turned by clues, stories, red herrings and motives – I have felt off balance. I never feel off balance,' said Bell. 'Something wasn't quite adding up. This seems so simple: a locked room, a closed circle of suspects, plentiful motives, an abundance of clues. But it was all too much. It seemed as though it was a set up in some way. As though there was a hand guiding – or indeed, pushing – us through this narrative. Someone is creating the perfect impenetrable crime. Everyone an archetype. All the usual tropes. Lots of boxes ticked. And then I thought, who could that hand belong to? Who could be the author of this piece?

'I have never been so fooled as I have in this case. Because I have been a fool. Such a fool. And I take the responsibility for being led. I have come to the very late realization that my hostess has deceived me.'

He stopped in front of Abigail.

'You are the murderer, Abigail,' Bell said simply. 'You killed your brother and then you invited me here to participate in this charade.'

'Absolutely ridiculous,' said Stephen. Margaret shook her head in disbelief. Barbara clutched the armchair rest. Cormac held Olivia close, and Declan let out a noise of surprise.

'It is not ridiculous, Stephen. It is very clear. Abigail knows what she has done.' Bell faced her again. 'You and you alone killed your brother. Whether out of spite or jealousy or greed or pure hatred. You did it, Abigail. You did it. It was your fault.'

And Abigail nearly admitted it.

PART THREE

'And, yes, his death has changed the story of his life. It has made it more mysterious. Not darker. I see as much light there as before. And standing before him, I do not search for what I might have foreseen and didn't – as if the essential was missing from what passed between us; rather I now begin with his violent death, and, from it, look back with increased tenderness on what he set out to do and what he offered to others, for as long as he could endure.'

A Fortunate Man: The Story of a Country Doctor,
JOHN BERGER (1967)

*

Their mother is calling them. 'Abigail. Benjamin.' She says their names as if it is a song. 'Time to go.' They hurry downstairs with their backpacks. They have all the usual things you would expect for a trip to the beach: buckets and spades, swimming costumes and towels. Their parents will bring sunscreen and hats they will force them to wear. Their father has already put a paddling board in the boot of the car and there are also books and a Walkman in case boredom sets in on the trip. Their mother has organized the food. Benjamin has brought the fishing net he got for his eighth birthday so that he can go exploring in the rock pools and Abigail has packed some of her most precious things that she can't bear being apart from: a small piece of shiny fabric, a bird feather and three purple buttons.

Their father is already in the driver's seat with all the doors open and the radio on. His legs hang out the side. The boot is open, and they pile their bags and towels and sunscreen and picnic into it. Doors bang shut, their father reverses onto the road and they are off.

Their mother keeps her window open and the wind whips through the car, causing her hair to fly about her face. Her eyes are closed behind her sunglasses and her skin is already brown from the summer sun. Their father turns up the volume on the radio. In the back seat Abigail and Benjamin are discussing in detail what they plan to do once they get to the beach.

They will go swimming first, they decide. They might swim again later on, especially if it is very hot and they need to cool down, but they will definitely swim first and then make a sandcastle. Benjamin has been planning this sandcastle since their last trip to the beach. He has ambitious plans: a moat, towers, a castle on top of a hill. He has imagined a whole neighbourhood of smaller sandcastles. There will be a little village and bridges and flowing water. Of course, now that they think about it, maybe after they finish swimming and have dried off, they should have a snack and then go down to the rock pool. Yes, that would a better idea. There they would find nice stones and shells and seaweed to decorate their kingdom. At some point they would probably have the picnic with their parents – ham and tomato sandwiches, hunks of watermelon, hard-boiled eggs, and ice creams from the cooler – and then it would be back to the sandcastle building.

Abigail turns on her Walkman and presses her hand against the interior of the car door: it is oven-hot. She is listening to an audiobook her father bought her for Christmas. It is not the scary one that she has had to hide at the bottom of the wardrobe. It is the funny one that she plays most days.

For Abigail and Benjamin, the drive takes an indeterminable amount of time. It feels like half the day, though in reality, it is only slightly over an hour. In years to come they will drive down by themselves, realize how short a journey it is and wonder why they didn't come here every weekend.

The journey has its own rhythm: hedges, derelict pubs, sharp turns in the road and bungalows flash by in a familiar cadence. They stop at the same small shop so that their father can buy the paper. They hit traffic jams at the same places each time. And then the car slows down and makes the final turn, and they know they are nearly there. They start to sit up a little straighter. Abigail packs her Walkman away and starts to stretch her arms. Benjamin feels the excitement brewing in his fingertips and he turns to Abigail and grins.

It is quiet here, but it is always quiet. It is only a small cove and there are more popular spots nearby. For Benjamin and Abigail, the cove is all they have known, and they feel proprietorial over it. It is their place: the car park, the boardwalk down to the beach, the spot in the sand they lay their blankets on, the rock pool.

Their father pulls into the dusty car park, parks the car, and turns off the engine. Benjamin and Abigail want to run onto the beach immediately but instead they must wait patiently while their parents unpack the car. They are each given a load to carry. Abigail has the buckets and spades, and Benjamin brings the paddling board and towels.

The day falls into its usual pattern: their mother reminds them to be careful of other cars, but they pay little attention to her as they race through the car park and down the boardwalk, dumping their belongings in a spot just below the dunes. There are only a handful of other people around: an older couple on deck chairs, a man out swimming and a couple with a baby.

Their parents follow them slowly. Their mother holding her head up to the sun, their father laden down with picnic things. They spread out towels, set up the umbrella and unfold deck chairs. Benjamin and Abigail are impatient. They are raring to go but their father tells them to hold on for a moment. They can't yet go swimming by themselves. They will need to wait for him.

Abigail and Benjamin watch their toes sink into the sand until their father is ready and then they rush towards the sea. The water is shockingly cold against their shins, but they soon wade in until it's at their shoulders. They swim out as far as the buoy and then they bob, suddenly not feeling the cold anymore. The man who had been swimming has gone back to shore and is drying himself off. They are the only ones in the sea in any direction they look. Abigail can feel small fishes and seaweed brushing against her legs. She licks her lips, and they are salty.

Small white waves crash on the beach. They tell their father that they want to go surfing and so he goes back to the shore and retrieves the paddling board. He puts Abigail on it first and leads her further out into the sea. They wait there, baby waves causing them to bob until they see the first real swell. Then Abigail puts her torso flat on the board and starts to paddle madly until the wave catches her and carries her cleanly to the shoreline. Then they do it again and again. With each wave Abigail grows more confident. 'That was a big one!' she yells.

It is now Benjamin's turn. He has to wait a while for the next big wave. It is calm out today and he fears that Abigail has taken all the good waves for herself. But then they see it in the distance, rolling towards them, growing slowly bigger. Benjamin turns and starts to paddle fast. He feels the wave just behind him and then it starts to lift his legs then his torso and then in a final rush he is propelled toward the beach. 'That was the best one yet,' Abigail declares.

They continue like this while their father does laps, waiting patiently for the next wave and then taking turns surfing to the shoreline. They could do this for hours and hours, but their father tires sooner than they do and encourages them to come back to the beach so that he can lay down for a while and have a cool drink.

They have a race back to shore. Benjamin comes first, Abigail second and their father lags in third. They run to where their mother is and, suddenly cold, they cover themselves in towels and she rubs their backs and helps to dry their hair. Their skin smells of summer: warm sun cream and sea salt. They recount their surfing adventures to their mother, who listens patiently.

Once they are ready, they pull T-shirts over their now-dry swimming costumes and, armed with buckets and nets, they go to their little rock pool. There they find a starfish with only four arms. 'They can grow their arms back,' says Benjamin, who has recently learned this fact in school. Because Abigail is only five and a bit and won't start school until September, she thinks Benjamin is an otherworldly genius and believes everything he says. Benjamin bends down and picks up the starfish gently like he has seen them do at the aquarium. 'Do you want to touch it?' he asks Abigail. He holds the creature out for her, and she brushes it gently. It doesn't feel like she was expecting. It is hard and leathery, and it makes her squirm inside. After Benjamin places the starfish carefully back into the rock pool, he gathers some seaweed and puts it into Abigail's bucket. She puts her hand in, and it is slimy. There are all sorts of interesting shells about: pearlescent spirals, shiny broken shards, and perfect brilliant whites. She watches as Benjamin collects them and then places them carefully on top of the seaweed in her bucket. She picks out a particularly iridescent one. 'I want this one for my sandcastle,' she says. 'We need some stones,' he tells her, and they continue to trawl the beach. Once their buckets are full, they return to their parents.

Their mother wants to cover them with sunscreen again, and they dutifully allow her to rub the sticky cream onto their backs. But they are itching to start their build. 'Keep an eye on your sister,' their father tells Benjamin, and of course he will. They pick up their bright plastic buckets and walk down towards the sea where the sand has been soaked with salt water and fill their buckets tightly with the cement. They then carry them back to their building site. Benjamin helps Abigail with her load because he is her big brother. They pat down the sand and then carefully – very carefully – Benjamin turns the bucket over in one fell swoop. They tap on the base of the bucket – twice from Benjamin and twice from Abigail; they have perfected the system. Benjamin then lifts the bucket to reveal a perfectly moulded sandcastle. He looks towards Abigail excitedly and she claps in celebration. It is still a small miracle every time this happens. Then he picks up Abigail's bucket and they go through the same routine. Abigail runs to retrieve her beautiful shell fragment and places it daintily on top of this second sandcastle. She looks to Benjamin for approval.

They get another bucket – the smallest one – and create simpler outposts on either side of their two mansions. They begin to form mountains – piling mounds of sand up high. They create little paths between the two castles and trace doors onto the smaller sandcastles with their fingers. Abigail starts decorating because that is her favourite part. She uses all the best stones and shells for herself, and haphazardly strews seaweed over her kingdom. Benjamin collects more sand to build up the walls around the two castles. He does this because he is older and stronger than Abigail and it is heavy work carrying wet sand back and forth. He forms the curved walls carefully with his hands until they are sturdy, and he is happy with them.

Benjamin tracks a path for the moat around the two castles, his bare hands furrowing through the warm sand. Then they start to dig, first scraping with plastic spades and then scooping out with their hands. They work quickly, only stopping when their mother calls them to have their picnic. Once they're full they run back to their sandcastle kingdom and continue to dig out the moat. Since they have been on the beach some people have left and one or two others have arrived.

Finally, the moat is complete, and Benjamin goes searching for appropriately large flat stones to be used as the draw-bridges on either side. They've been learning about medieval castles at school and so he knows all about drawbridges and battlements and why soldiers slept upright in bed.

He takes an empty bucket and goes down towards the sea. His eyes are glued to the sand. He finds a good shell and a nice piece of hazy green glass that he knows Abigail will like.

There is a lot of seaweed everywhere. He walks along the shoreline until he finally finds the exact type of stone he is looking for: pale and flat and big as his palm. He finds another one: slightly fatter but it will do. He puts it in his bucket with everything else and then starts to truck back to his parents and sister and the sandcastle kingdom.

He is a little tired by the time he gets back but thankfully it is time for ice cream. His father opens the large cooler and hands them out. He sits on the sand with Abigail next to their construction site and they silently eat their choc ices. Soon there is ice cream dripping down the hands of Benjamin and Abigail and onto the sand. They rush to the sea where they wave their fingers through the water until they are cool and clean again. Then Benjamin dries Abigail's small hands with his T-shirt.

They return to the sandcastle. Benjamin carefully sets the drawbridge in place and then rearranges the seaweed strewn by Abigail earlier. He likes things to be a certain way. Small stones become pathways and turrets and windows. It is difficult to get some of the stones to stay in place. A couple of the windows have already fallen out. Benjamin starts a repair job on some of them: he gently digs out a small amount of sand and then pushes the stone windows into place. Abigail is very impressed and is even more impressed when he presents her with the piece of green glass he has found. She stores this jewel carefully in the front pocket of her bag. Later, when she is at home, she will place it with her other precious things in what she believes is her secret place: a drawer in her nightstand that her mother has nightmares about. Occasionally, their mother has to throw things out when they start to become a genuine health hazard. But also, when she is at home by herself, she takes a peek to make herself smile.

Once they are happy with their masterpiece, they invite their parents to survey it. Their mother and father coo and aww at this fantastic feat of engineering. They admire the moat and Abigail makes sure that they know she helped to dig it out. She points out the pretty shell to them and how she has laid out the seaweed in elaborate patterns to signify lush lawns and flowers. They are very impressed.

Abigail is finished with the sandcastle now and goes and sits in the shade to listen to her Walkman and examine the piece of glass Benjamin had given her. Benjamin stays with the sandcastle to perfect it further. He smooths the sides of the moat. He repositions the drawbridge. He moves seaweed. He gets a bucket and goes down to the sea where he fills it up with water. He carries it back with two hands and has to stop halfway to put the bucket down and rub his arms. He watches his parents and sister from afar and it is like they are in a postcard.

He pours the water into the moat, where it just sinks into the sand. Benjamin gets down on his hands and knees to inspect it. He places his hand into the now saturated sand and pushes it down until it is fully compacted. He tries again: goes to the sea, collects seawater – his arms hurt a lot now, but it will be worth it – and tries to fill up the moat. But it is no use. The water just disappears. He realizes that he is out of his depth and so he asks his father for help. 'How do I fill up the moat?' he asks. 'How do I get the water to stay put?' His father puts his paper down and comes to inspect the issue. 'You see, the problem is that you have no proper foundation.

If you were building a swimming pool, say, you would have to dig out the hole and then line it with something and tile it or whatever and then the water can't get through. That's why the water just soaks into the sand,' his father explains. 'What can I line it with?' His father looks around. 'I'm not sure we have anything with us. We'll have to remember it for next time,' he says. 'You could collect some blueish rocks to make it look like water,' he suggests. Benjamin gets his bucket again. 'Where are you going?' asks Abigail, suddenly interested. 'I have to find enough stones to fill this whole moat,' says Benjamin. 'I'll come too,' Abigail says, and she hands her Walkman to her mother for safe keeping. 'I have to go help Benjamin, but I'll be back soon,' she assures her mother. Benjamin tells her to take a bucket as well. 'We need a lot of small stones. We need to fill up the entire moat,' he says. They go back towards the boardwalk, as this area has the most stones. Abigail puts down her bucket and tries to pick up a huge rock with both her hands. She pushes and pulls but it barely moves. 'What about this one?' she asks. 'You'll have to pick it up though. It hurts my hands.' 'No, we need small ones,' explains Benjamin. 'Like pebbles. See, like this.'

On the other side of the boardwalk, he finds a cluster of smaller blueish-grey stones and starts to put these in his bucket. He won't have enough, he thinks to himself. He has a strong image in his head now of what this moat should look like, and he will be disappointed if it does not live up to his expectations. Abigail isn't helping anymore. She has become distracted by a sand insect she is trying to trap. She is crouched down close to the ground, her face scrunched-up and focused as the little insect or whatever it is hops about. She cups her hands around him, but he hops out of reach. She falls over and has to right herself. She watches him keenly, but he is quick and manages to escape from her grasp yet again. She crouches down further and makes herself very still. She waits patiently, and suddenly and silently envelopes the insect in her finger prison. He is tickling her. She wonders if she would be able to hold him all the way home in the car. Maybe if she was very careful. If she gets him home, she could keep him in her bedroom as a pet. She slowly stands up with her palms still clasped and picks her way across the boardwalk. She doesn't want to fall and crush him, or even worse, let him go. Benjamin is still diligently collecting pebbles.

Abigail carefully makes her way back to where her parents are sitting. She finds that she can't sit down easily while her hands are clasped like this. This isn't going to be as easy as she thinks. How will she pack her bag? Her mother is watching her suspiciously. 'What have you got there?' her mother calls. 'Nothing,' she says and then releases her hands to destroy the evidence. She will have to be sneakier next time. Then she remembers what she is supposed to be doing and runs back to join Benjamin on the other side of the boardwalk, following him around and picking up stones haphazardly. 'I think we have enough now,' says Abigail once she is bored, and they go back to the sandcastles.

Benjamin starts to pour the stones into the gully and instructs Abigail to do the same, but she has started yawning and that means the day must be nearly over. Benjamin could continue on like this for hours. He has about a third of the moat covered with pebbles before the tide is suddenly upon him. The water ripples threateningly. He feels it at his heels. It finally reaches the edge of the moat and water pours into the gully. Their parents are calling to them. It is time to pack up and go. Abigail runs to get her things, but Benjamin waits behind to watch the ocean devour his creation. It comes again and his feet are underwater. It is getting closer to the sandcastles. He wishes he could wrap them up and take them home with him. His father calls him again and he has to go. He packs up his bag and stands watching as the water gets closer and closer. He feels powerless but he can't look away. Then suddenly a final push and the water has engulfed everything. When it retreats it leaves behind an ugly lumpen mound of wet sand. He will just have to make a better one next time.

The day is over.

They roll up their towels, collect their rubbish and left-over food, and close the umbrella. Benjamin helps to carry the now-empty cooler: he has one handle; his father has the other. There is nothing left behind that would indicate they were ever there. They walk back up the boardwalk towards their car and pack everything into the boot. The car is baking hot, so they open all the doors and sit there while they pour sand out of their shoes and air out the towels. Their father turns on the radio as their mother lowers herself into the passenger seat. They discuss between them whether this was the best day they've had down here weather-wise and reminisce about previous visits: two years ago, when it started to rain on the way down; five years ago, when Abigail was just a baby and they underestimated how difficult it would be with a toddler and a baby on the beach. They close the car doors and roll down the windows and their father backs out of the parking space. His hands on the steering wheel are red. Their mother's hair whips around. Abigail is yawning. Benjamin is still thinking about his sandcastles. They are going home.

ACKNOWLEDGEMENTS

Angelique Tran Van Sang, Allison Malecha, Anne Meadows, Rosie Shackles, Mary Mount, Kieran Sangha, Emily Griffin, Noah Eaker, everyone at Picador, everyone at Harper, Mom, Dad and Martha.

Thank you.